PORTRAIT OF A WOMAN AND JESUS

HE LOOKED THROUGH HER EYES AND INTO HER HEART

BY
BARBARA QUILLEN EGBERT

ARTWORK BY
WILSON ONG

Barbara Quillen Egbert

Jesus sees & knows you —
and He loves you!

Quillen Egbert, Barbara
Portrait of a Woman and Jesus: He Looked Through Her Eyes and into Her Heart

ISBN: 978-096617355-0
LCCN: 2011927656

Artwork: Wilson Ong
Cover and book design: John Egbert
Layout design: Cardinal Graphics & Design
Published by: New Voice Publications
                            PO Box 14133
                            Irvine, CA 92623

PORTRAIT OF A WOMAN AND JESUS
HE LOOKED THROUGH HER EYES AND INTO HER HEART

Dedicated to my daughter Brittany:

May you come to know within the depths of your heart how dearly loved you are by Jesus.

Acknowledgements

- To Wendy Bjurstrom and Cheryl Brasuell for launching this journey with their prayers requesting unveiling and usefulness.

- To my devoted husband Jeb Egbert for gracious encouragement during the creative process and for financial support.

- To my dear mother Lois Quillen, Nancy Egbert and Lorraine Pelly who have mentored me through life while modeling and sharing valuable insights.

- To my family and numerous friends (specifically Cindy Bauter, Sarah Miles, Patricia Miller, Shelly Houston, Winifred Gahm, Wendy Hubbard, Deb Griffith, Kathleen Rodarte, Michelle Woroniecki, Debbie Watts and Susan Rohrer and Laura Urista) for their prayers, words of encouragement and editorial suggestions.

- To Elizabeth and Marcus Plourde whom God miraculously placed in my path to give an unknown writer a voice.

- To Wilson Ong, the talented artist whom God provided to partner in this project.

- To my son John Egbert and John O'Dell for using their God-given talent to create a book more beautiful than I imagined.

- To my heavenly Father for giving me the vision for this book and for providing inspiration and guidance each step of the way. Thank You for choosing me to share the story of Your Son.

PORTRAIT OF A WOMAN AND JESUS

HE LOOKED THROUGH HER EYES AND INTO HER HEART

PREFACE

My spiritual journey has been fueled by a quest to understand and experience the love of our heavenly Father and His Son. One interpretation of the ministry of Jesus that forever changed my awareness of God's incomprehensible love and compassion for humanity was presented in the film The Gospel of Matthew. The portrayal of Jesus by actor Bruce Marchiano came to life as the settings, cultural background, clothing and people were captured on film.

The scenes in The Gospel of Matthew that captivated my heart and forever changed the way I viewed Jesus were the ones when He was interacting face-to-face with people. Jesus' encounters with individuals and the expression of exuberant joy that He displayed after providing for their needs — whether as Healer, Redeemer, Forgiver, Comforter and ultimately as Savior — showed His intimacy with the human heart and genuine care for each person.

Though the ultimate saving act on the cross fulfilled Jesus' purpose for mankind, it was through the saving acts on a day-to-day level that He also demonstrated His encompassing love. These daily interactions expressed His understanding of our desire to live this physical life to the full while anticipating eternal life with God.

WHAT TO EXPECT FROM THIS BOOK

This book is written as a discovery of the lives of women as they were impacted by a relationship with Jesus. We will see a variety of situational relationships with Jesus — from strangers who sought out Jesus, to those He encountered during daily events, to those in His inner circle of friends and family. Each portrait is intended to help the reader connect heart-to-heart with the women Jesus encountered and witness the goodness of His heart. We will be reminded of the multifaceted roles that Jesus plays in our lives that are specific to our heart's needs and desires and see Jesus as our Healer, Redeemer, Teacher, Savior, Comforter and Friend.

Psalm 103:2-5 NIV complements the vision of this book:
"Praise the Lord, O my soul,
and forget not all his benefits —
who forgives all your sins
and heals all your diseases,
who redeems your life from the pit
and crowns you with love and compassion,
who satisfies your desires with good things
so that your youth is renewed like the eagle's."

Each woman in these portraits was the beneficiary of a brief, yet intimate encounter with Jesus. She was impacted by His spoken words of truth and she experienced one or more of His characteristics. Scripture was fulfilled in a personal and unique way for her.

As you put yourself into the sandals of the Biblical women Jesus encountered, I pray that you will begin to relate more completely to each woman and grasp, to a greater degree, His desire to deepen His relationship with you! Out of His limitless love and ability to look through your eyes and into the depths of your heart, Jesus will interact with you on an intimately personal level. He will meet your unique needs and desires.

INTRODUCTION

THE VISION OF THIS BOOK

As a woman, I am drawn to the accounts involving women in the Bible and am specifically interested in Jesus' interaction with them during His brief ministry on this earth. Though living in a different place and time, I have begun to identify with these women in their unique situations and can empathize with the cries of their hearts. I have a growing understanding of the impact Jesus' interactions made on each woman and how He challenged cultural norms regarding women. Jesus' response to each of these women were statements of who He was and is, revealing His character and heart, confirming that the Son of God's purpose was all about loving humans individually and giving them life.

One morning as several components of my life journey combined into a vivid vision, a personal portrait came to mind that was intimately expressive of my own unique heart. I began to envision what a portrait of each Biblical woman's encounter with Jesus would look like based on the one God had given me. Thus, the idea for the book was born.

This book is written by a woman, from a woman's perspective and includes only the stories of Jesus' interactions with women. My intent is to capture verbally and visually a "snapshot" of each face-to-face encounter, as if looking through her eyes and into her heart. What would it have been like to be a bystander so many generations ago and actually witness the scene? What emotions would Jesus have seen in each woman's heart? Can we identify with the woman's life and appreciate the impact Jesus had on her? What are some of the timeless lessons we can learn from Jesus' responses to each woman's situation?

We will witness Jesus' intent and love for the woman He encountered and transfer it to our own lives, gaining a deeper awareness of Jesus' zealous love for us. What needs and desires are compelling us to reach out to Jesus and ask for intervention? By reading about His responses to the various women, we can gain confidence in His ability to satisfy us, as well. How do we respond when Jesus interacts with us? We will see how the women in these stories displayed joy, gratitude, praise and service. These enduring examples will encourage us to respond from our hearts after Jesus has impacted our lives.

PORTRAIT OF AN ENCOUNTER WITH JESUS

The portraits included in this book are designed to capture a moment in Biblical time when a woman was personally affected by an interaction or relationship with Jesus. We have attempted to both verbally and visually portray each encounter to reflect what each woman might have experienced during the meeting. Some details that surround the event are provided for us, but there are others that we can only imagine. Every portrait begins with a scriptural paraphrase of the encounter. The various Gospel accounts are combined into one reading that includes all aspects of the recorded meeting between Jesus and each specific woman. The New International Version (NIV), Contemporary English Version (CEV) and Holman Christian Standard Bible (HCSB) were used for the combined paraphrases. The descriptive representation of each event includes:

THE SCENE

A description is provided as the scene between the woman and Jesus developed. As we were not present at the actual event, thoughts are based on the few details given to us in Scripture as well as cultural clues and the author's intuitive explorations and fictional enhancements of the woman's circumstances. If we witnessed the developing scenario, what might we see? What details are important to include? What would be the mood? Who would be there with this woman? What are the circumstances that brought this woman into close proximity to Jesus?

JESUS LOOKED INTO HER HEART

It has been said that "the eyes are the mirror into the soul," conveying the emotions of the heart. During every encounter between Jesus and the woman in the Biblical account, there was a moment, brief or lingering, when Jesus looked directly at her. The visual portrait by Wilson Ong captures this "snapshot" of when the eyes of Jesus and the woman met. It is at that split second of a moment when He looked through her eyes and into her heart.

We can only attempt to imagine what Jesus perceived in each woman, but historical and scriptural clues, as well as the ability to "put ourselves into His and her shoes," will help us. What emotion of the woman, the subject of the scene, has been portrayed? Is it a moment of denial, guilt, deceit, grief, desperation, embarrassment or joy? Artist Wilson Ong has attempted to capture the action, mood and facial expressions of this particular moment, as frozen in time.

HIS RESPONSE

Jesus, as the Son of God, is the only One who is able to intimately look into the depths of a woman's heart and know all of her needs and desires. He alone has the power to touch a woman's heart and heal, restore, forgive, rescue and satisfy. After identifying each woman's specific need or request, Jesus responded. Some needed physical healing; others needed spiritual forgiveness. His varied responses to each woman testified to who He was and is, His will, what motivates Him, His mission on earth and the plan for humanity.

THE OUTCOME

A woman can learn to conceal the innermost depths of her heart. Over time she may unknowingly have buried emotions, feelings, desires and questions that relate to her identity. But after experiencing Jesus' look into the depths of her heart, with His accompanying intervention, a woman's life is changed forever. Each of the outcomes shows the complete power of Jesus, as Son of God, to impact an individual life in dynamic and tangible ways while challenging cultural and religious norms.

As we see the spontaneous reactions and outcome from those who were blessed by their encounter with Jesus, we will be reminded of the natural response to His graceful and merciful hand on our own lives. The Lord was praised and worshipped by many women. They followed and served Him in return for the unwavering love shown to them.

PORTRAIT OF A WOMAN AND JESUS

HE LOOKED THROUGH HER EYES AND INTO HER HEART

THE WOMAN WHO TOUCHED JESUS

A large crowd was following and pressing against Him. In the crowd was a woman who had been bleeding for twelve years, but no one could heal her. She had suffered a great deal under the care of many doctors and had spent all she had. But instead of getting better, she only got worse.

Having heard about Jesus, she came up behind Him in the crowd and touched His robe. She had said to herself, "If I can just touch His robe, I'll be made well!" Immediately her bleeding stopped and she felt in her body that she was freed from her suffering.

At once Jesus realized in Himself that power had gone out from Him. So He was looking around to see who had done this. He turned around in the crowd and asked, "Who touched Me?"

While everyone around was denying it, Peter said, "Master, the crowds are hemming You in and pressing against You and You ask, 'Who touched Me?'"

"Somebody did touch Me," said Jesus. "I know that power has gone out from Me."

Jesus turned and saw her. The woman knew that she could not hide. Knowing what had happened to her, she came with fear and trembling, fell down before Him, and told Him the whole truth. In the presence of all the people, she declared the reason she had touched Him and how she was instantly cured.

"Have courage, daughter," He said to her, "your faith has healed you. Go in peace and be freed from your suffering."

YOUR
FAITH HAS
HEALED
YOU.

MATTHEW 9:20-22
MARK 5:24-34
LUKE 8:42-48

THE SCENE

Clutching the shawl tightly around her head, a woman discretely made her way through the crowd, avoiding eye contact with anyone she might have known. Why did she want to go unnoticed? She had been suffering the indignity and embarrassment of chronic bleeding for twelve years!

Every disability or disease brings a particular set of challenges and heartbreak. But a woman with a hemorrhage was probably impacted more severely than if she had a different ailment. According to Jewish law, when a woman bleeds from the womb she is considered "unclean." Everything and anyone she touches during her time of bleeding is infected with uncleanness as well.

Imagine this woman's despair after suffering for twelve years! She was probably shunned and ostracized. She lived an isolated social life of humiliation, not allowed to worship or enjoy a natural friendship with others. Not only did bleeding cause a major inconvenience, it also affected her entire health. She suffered from chronic low physical energy and possibly from anemia.

This woman may have been single, potentially dooming her to poverty and loneliness. If she were married, there must have been considerable strain on her relationship. Most likely she was unable to have children. In a society that equated a woman's worth with the ability to produce children, this hemorrhaging could have had accompanying emotional feelings of uselessness, as well as deep depression.

Placing her hope in doctors was futile. They had provided no answers, but depleted her financial resources in her quest for healing. Her physical situation worsened and her anguish reached the desperation point. She overheard stories of a man named Jesus who had healing power and was in town. He was her last and only hope!

Though it was a risk to be seen publicly or to touch anyone, she was compelled to search for Jesus. She must find Him! Maybe He will heal me, she thought. She was hopeful that the number of people hurrying to see Him would aid her desire for obscurity. She felt so insignificant and worthless, not wanting to bother Him. She did not pursue a spoken word or even a visual acknowledgement from Him. Instead, she determined to inconspicuously touch His clothes, believing that He had the power to restore her health and make her "clean."

That must be Jesus! Inching her way through the crowd she boldly moved right behind Him, reached out and gently touched His garment. Instantly, she sensed that her bleeding had stopped and reflexively gasped as she felt strength and wholeness wash over her body for the first time in twelve years! Barely grasping the reality of the miracle, she was jolted by Jesus' reaction.

He immediately turned around and asked, "Who touched Me?" because He knew healing power had gone out from Him. Instead of walking away and letting her experience the miracle privately, Jesus set up an encounter that would provide a witness to the crowd.

Jesus continued to pursue the issue of who had touched Him, looking around at those surrounding Him. However, all were denying it. Though the woman tried to avoid His searching look, their eyes met and she could no longer go unnoticed. She fell at His feet, trembling with fear as she told Him the whole truth.

JESUS LOOKED INTO HER HEART

Why would Jesus be looking into eyes filled with fear? Maybe this woman felt guilty to have touched Him in her "unclean" state. Or maybe she felt she would be met with a rebuke for seeking Him in a secretive manner. Perhaps she feared the repercussions when it was discovered that she had broken a religious requirement. But instead of rebuke or anger, Jesus extended His hand in a reassuring gesture and listened as she told her story.

She shared the deepest part of her heart—the pain, suffering, embarrassment and rejection that she had endured for years! She also confessed why she had sought Him out anonymously and confirmed that she had been instantly healed. This ultimately became a public declaration of her faithful heart and Jesus' healing power.

By confronting this woman face-to-face, Jesus gave those present an opportunity to hear her story and to witness His loving response. Though Jesus was on His way to attend to the ill daughter of a prominent synagogue official, He graciously took the time to address an ordinary woman's undeniable need. By acknowledging this woman, merely one woman in the crowd, Jesus demonstrated that each individual matters.

HIS RESPONSE

After listening to her story, maybe spoken with a trembling voice as tears ran down her cheeks, He responded with words that elevated her humble status to one of favor, calling her "daughter," indicating her restoration to full identity in the community. He revealed to the crowd that her example of faith had healed her and she was now freed from suffering. He also calmed her fears by telling her to "go in peace."

What a response! An instant healing! Jesus gave the cure that she had sought in vain from doctors for twelve years. Not only was she healed physically, but Jesus also publicly restored her reputation in a profound way. Formerly perceived as "unclean," she received words of favor in front of the crowd she had previously avoided.

Instead of treating her with disdain, Jesus' interaction was done out of kindness and understanding. While initially it may have seemed harsh to force the issue of determining who had touched His robe, it was only through the immediacy of the healing touch and outpouring of her heart that the encounter could have the greatest impact on those who were gathered around. With a joyful smile, He released her from suffering and gave her peace. Jesus was her Healer, Savior and Redeemer. She had directly received His restoring power from just one touch.

THE OUTCOME

This woman's life would never be the same after she touched Jesus' clothes. Jesus restored her health and standing in society's eyes, freeing her from years of hopelessness. Gone was the shame, replaced by confirmation that she was loved and valued in Jesus' eyes. He took the time to listen to her heart and responded completely to her need and desire to be healed.

Freedom from suffering! Physically she would be able to function normally as a woman again. If single, would she be able to pursue marriage? Would she be able to have children now? No longer was life dictated by the limitations of a physical ailment. Now she was able to move forward with plans for her life.

We can only imagine the emotional freedom that she would also experience. Freedom from shame, from withdrawal! She had renewed hope for her future and was able to enjoy relationships again because she was now considered "clean." Formerly ostracized, she would be socially accepted and could hold in her heart the words of special favor spoken by Jesus. What a contrast to live with joy instead of suffering and with dignity instead of shame.

What was it like to actually touch Jesus' garment and suddenly feel the healing power of restoration? What a story she had to share with others! Would she now walk with a smile on her face and with thankfulness and praise in her heart for the One she had directly encountered? Did she touch others with similar mercy and grace she was given?

Though this woman reached out to Jesus, it was her faith in Him that brought healing. We are not in proximity to Jesus as she was, but faith in His power still heals and restores. He knows your needs! Be encouraged to approach Jesus with confidence and boldness, trusting in His eternal goodness toward you.

Eventually this woman died. Jesus' power will restore her again — to a new and eternal life, where suffering and death cannot exist.

"ARE NOT FIVE SPARROWS SOLD FOR TWO PENNIES? YET NOT ONE OF THEM IS FORGOTTEN BY GOD. INDEED, THE VERY HAIRS OF YOUR HEAD ARE ALL NUMBERED. DON'T BE AFRAID; YOU ARE WORTH MORE THAN MANY SPARROWS."

Luke 12:6-7 NIV

A GRIEVING MOTHER

Jesus went to a town called Nain. His disciples and a large crowd were traveling with Him. As they came near the gate of the town, a dead man was being carried out. He was his mother's only son, and she was a widow. Many people from the town were walking along with her. When the Lord saw the woman, He had compassion on her and said, "Don't cry."

Then He came up and touched the open coffin, and those carrying it stood still. He said, "Young man, I say to you, get up!" The dead man sat up and began to speak, and Jesus gave him back to his mother.

They were all filled with awe and praised God, saying, "A great prophet has appeared among us," and, "God has come to help His people." This news about Jesus spread throughout Judea and everywhere else in that part of the country.

DON'T CRY.

THE SCENE

The funeral procession with accompanying sounds of weeping and wailing was impossible to ignore. As Jesus and those traveling with Him were approaching the entrance to the city, their smiles and friendly conversations began to subside. It soon became clear that a large crowd from the town was escorting a woman and the body of her dead son to the burial grounds. They respectfully stepped aside to let the grieving procession pass.

We are not given specific details on the status of this woman, the age of her son or how he died. We do know that he was her only son and she was a widow. Many neighbors supported her through this tragic time, surrounding her with comforting arms. With the loss of her husband, and now her only son, this woman's situation looked hopeless and her audible mourning expressed the depth of her grief.

It only took one look for Jesus' heart to be touched by the double tragedy this woman was experiencing, and He stepped toward the open coffin. Those carrying the lifeless body hesitated and then stopped, sensing the presence of a man with authority. Confused, the downcast woman looked up at the man standing in front of her.

JESUS LOOKED INTO HER HEART

As Jesus looked through her eyes, He perceived a heart aching from profound grief. First she lost her husband and became a widow, and now she lost her only son. She had nothing left. Perhaps she feared what her future would now bring. Maybe she lost all will to continue on. Jesus could see into the depths of her anguish and hopelessness.

In her culture, a widow without a man to provide for her needs would likely become destitute, as she probably would be unable to earn a living for herself. Jesus would have been aware of the vulnerability of her impending poverty from losing her husband and son. Not only would the physical challenge of survival be severe, but the emotional outcome of her double loss was devastating. His heart went out to her, motivating Him to rescue her from the seemingly inevitable pit of loneliness that she now faced.

Maybe Jesus projected forward to the time when His own widowed mother would be grieving in a similar way for the loss of her son — an event that only He could foresee. His heart overflowed with empathy.

HIS RESPONSE

"Don't cry," He tenderly said. These words were not spoken to diminish her expression of grief or to minimize the emotional impact of her suffering, but were spoken out of compassion to convey comfort and hope. These reassuring words reflected a time in the future when "He will wipe away every tear from their eyes. There will be no more death or mourning or crying or pain, for the old order of things has passed away" (Revelation 21:4 NIV).

Though the coffin would have been considered unclean by Jewish Law, Jesus' compassion for this woman who had previously buried her husband and was about to bury her only son compelled Him to reach out and touch it. Jesus commanded the young man to get up!

The crowd was shocked to see the dead man sit up and talk! With tears in His eyes and a smile on His face, Jesus helped the bewildered man off the coffin platform and into his mother's open arms. Sounds of crying were replaced by expressions of shock and amazement and with shouts of praise and reverence. Soon boisterous chatter filled the air. Tears of grief turned to tears of joy as the reality began to sink in that they had just witnessed the restoration of this dead man! Imagine this mother's astonishment! Her only son was alive again!

Jesus' heart for widows and for those dealing with the loss of a child moved Him to raise a young man from the dead. Though the restored life was what the crowd was focused on, the impact on the individual woman was the most profound. This miracle demonstrated Jesus' kindhearted love for one grieving woman who faced an uncertain future without husband or son.

THE OUTCOME

Can you imagine the feelings this woman experienced? Her son was now fully alive! Was it all a dream? Who was this man who had so graciously restored her son to life? After the shock subsided, maybe the woman would focus on the events of the day. Who was this man who dared to touch a coffin, did not shun death and spoke life into a dead body? Why would He choose to revive her son? It was just too good to be true! Yet, it was only through the confirmation of her vibrant son and amazed friends that she realized that life had truly begun again.

The entire region was talking about this great prophet who appeared among them, but only she would appreciate the personal nature of the miracle that had been performed. It was witnessed by the masses, but was understood as an individual act of compassion for an anonymous woman.

Would she see Jesus again? Maybe. Maybe not. Regardless of whether she faced him again, she would confidently testify about the power and love of this man named Jesus, who looked with kindness upon a poor widow and comforted her with grace. Instead of facing a life of loneliness and uncertainty, she now felt safe and secure.

This blessed woman most likely lived with an inner joy birthed by a consuming awareness that Jesus redeemed her from a seemingly hopeless pit and crowned her with love through His compassionate miracle of the restoration of her son. Truly, God had come to her aid in a powerful and personal way.

"I ASSURE YOU: AN HOUR IS COMING, AND IS NOW HERE, WHEN THE DEAD WILL HEAR THE VOICE OF THE SON OF GOD, AND THOSE WHO HEAR WILL LIVE."

John 5:25 HCSB

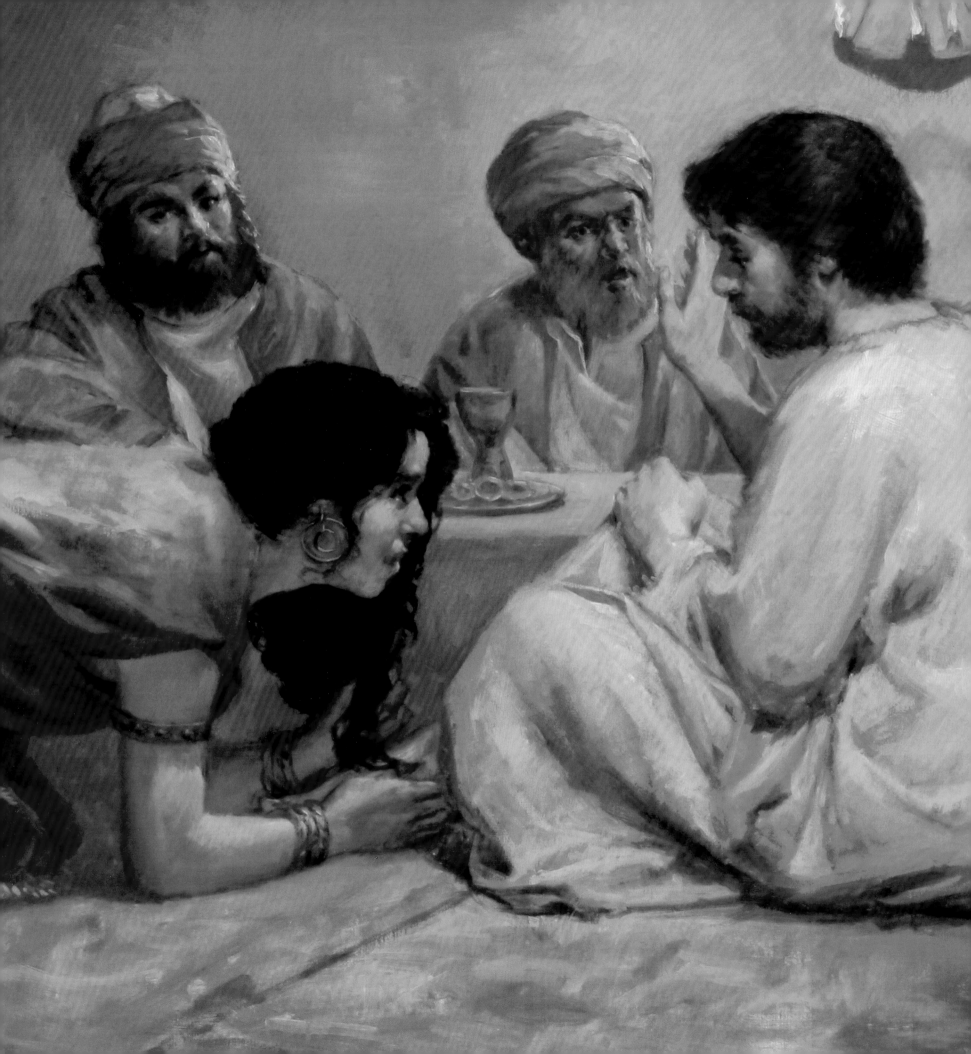

THE WOMAN WHO LOVED MUCH

Now one of the Pharisees invited Jesus to have dinner with him, so He entered the Pharisee's house and got ready to eat. When a woman who had lived a sinful life in that town learned that Jesus was eating at the Pharisee's house, she brought an alabaster flask of fragrant oil and stood behind Him at His feet, weeping. She began to wash His feet with her tears. She wiped His feet with her hair, kissing them and anointing them with the perfume.

When the Pharisee who had invited Jesus saw this he said to himself, "This man, if He were a prophet, would know who and what kind of woman this is who is touching Him — she's a sinner!"

Jesus replied to him, "Simon, I have something to say to you." "Tell me, teacher," he said. "Two people were in debt to a moneylender. One of them owed him five hundred silver coins, and the other owed him fifty. Since they could not pay it back, he graciously canceled the debts of both. So, which of them will love him more?"

Simon answered, "I suppose it would be the one who had owed more and didn't have to pay it back." "You have judged correctly," Jesus said.

Turning to the woman, He said to Simon, "Do you see this woman? I entered your house; you gave Me no water for My feet, but she has washed My feet with her tears and wiped them with her hair. You gave Me no kiss, but this woman, from the time I entered, has not stopped kissing My feet. You didn't anoint My head with oil, but she has anointed My feet with perfume. Therefore I tell you that her many sins are forgiven — for she loved much. But the one who is forgiven little, loves little."

Then Jesus said to the woman, "Your sins are forgiven." The other guests began to say among themselves, "Who is this man who dares to forgive sins?" Jesus said to the woman, "Your faith has saved you; go in peace."

YOUR
SINS
ARE
FORGIVEN.

LUKE 7:36-50

THE SCENE

A nameless woman heard that Jesus would be dining that evening at the home of Simon, a Pharisee. She must go to Him! Her desire to see Jesus was not borne out of a physical need such as a healing, and she did not have a request to make on behalf of a close family member. This yearning to be with Him was an intensely personal one that sprang from a heart convicted of her brokenness. Her deepest need was for forgiveness, which she believed He could bestow.

Though probably known by Simon, he certainly had not invited her, a woman AND a sinner. Regardless, she was determined to find Jesus. She knew that she would not be welcomed by Simon and his guests. In fact, she expected to be met with resistance because of her reputation in the town.

This woman was publicly branded as a sinner. Though the Biblical account does not specify how she received that status, most traditional interpretations of this story are quick to label this woman a prostitute. Though every person falls woefully short of perfection (thus, all have sinned), a prostituted woman would be an easy target of human condemnation because of her outwardly visible and identifiable failings. Because humans tend to classify sins and the degree of sinfulness, this woman was judged as an obvious sinner.

Those who were invited to the dinner gave disapproving stares as she approached. Simon's guests were not eager to cause a scene in front of Jesus, so they reluctantly allowed her to enter.

This marked woman was probably no stranger to abuse at the hands of men. So why would she seek out this man — Jesus? Maybe she had previously watched Him from afar and noticed that Jesus was profoundly different than any man she knew. He spoke with kindness and respect to every person, and surprisingly, He treated women with dignity. She was so tired of masking her shame, self-condemnation and loathing for the pit of existence she called life. Even though she felt unworthy and incapable of being "fixed," desperation fueled her search.

After finding Jesus at the table, she stood behind Him and quietly began to weep, her tears dripping down on His robe and feet. Her heart was overwhelmed with conviction of her human weakness and obvious flaws. She desperately wanted a new life. In an act of repentance and contrition she surrendered her regrets, mistakes and failed efforts at the feet of the One and only perfect being — the only One who had the love and power to forgive. Then she wept more, this time with gratitude.

This emotional outpouring was disconcerting for the host, but it was the intimacy of her proceeding actions that was shocking. Removing the covering of her head, this scorned woman wiped Jesus' moist feet with her hair, kissed them and then poured expensive perfume on them. To Simon, this was scandalous! How could Jesus allow a woman, specifically a sinful and prostituted woman, to touch Him in this way?

Jesus was well aware of the judging hearts of those witnessing this display of affection. With words for all to hear, He proceeded to tell Simon a parable about a moneylender who cancelled debts of two men. Simon correctly stated that the man whose debt was larger would love the moneylender more than the man with a smaller debt. Jesus had set the stage to deliver a profound lesson of forgiveness.

While Jesus conversed with the host, it seemed as though He was ignoring the woman, not even acknowledging her actions, shocking as they seemed. Then He turned toward her and prepared to speak again. The woman briefly looked up into His eyes, then dropped her head and continued with humility in repentant worship.

JESUS LOOKED INTO HER HEART

In contrast to those in attendance at the dinner, Jesus had unique insight into this woman's heart and understanding of her motives. Looking through the sadness in her eyes, Jesus would have empathized with the despair brought about by selling one's body to be used for a man's pleasure. While others would assume that she willingly made a choice to become a prostitute, He alone would have perceived the circumstances which had drawn her into this demeaning lifestyle. Knowing that no woman ever dreams of or willingly seeks this powerless existence, His heart would ache for her rescue and restoration.

Jesus also understood the purity of her actions, which the other men judged to be indecent. Jesus saw a woman who had opened herself to public scrutiny with a display of emotional vulnerability. He could read her desperate and repentant heart and allowed this intimate expression of adoration.

It could be implied from the story that Jesus and she had previously met, and her sins were already forgiven. She understood that forgiveness by Jesus' grace and mercy was unearned and therefore, this expression of repentant worship was also an act of gratitude, a demonstration of the depth of her thankfulness to Jesus.

All sin, whether publicly visible or not, is a result of human nature straying or rebelling from God's will. This woman recognized her flawed nature and realized that there was nothing she could humanly do to measure up to the perfect and holy nature of God. Her conviction of sinfulness was intensified due to the public shame she endured. Jesus saw a woman emptied of herself, trusting Him to forgive and redeem. She was overwhelmed by His grace, compassion and mercy and worshipped at His feet.

His Response

Jesus challenged Simon to acknowledge "this woman" and recounted the acts of devotion she had shown. He pointed out that Simon, as host, did not even perform the basic courtesies for a guest, yet "this woman" went above and beyond in a display of affection. Though Simon may have judged her actions as immoral because of her tainted reputation, Jesus did not interpret "this woman's" display as sensual in nature, but as an intimate expression of spiritual worship. He elevated the status of "this woman" by drawing attention to her example of devotion.

Jesus did not make her feel embarrassed for expressing heartfelt gratitude or minimize her emotional outburst. Her tears did not intimidate him and He was comfortable with a woman, even this prostituted one, touching Him, though others considered her actions inappropriate. Jesus did not react to her reputation, or to her past, but saw her in the present, in her entirety — not solely as a woman, but as a worshipper with a heart's expression of thankfulness bubbling over into this intimate act of reverence.

Jesus made another shocking statement to Simon by announcing that her sins (which admittedly, were many) had been forgiven because "she loved much." Her demonstration of adoration was in response to forgiveness He could bestow and to the respect with which she was treated. With courage and boldness, this woman took the initiative to move toward Jesus, publicly worshipping and expressing her love toward Him while risking even greater adverse societal reaction.

Next, He addressed the woman by confirming that her "sins had been forgiven," not because of her actions, but because of who He is. Her faith in Him had saved her. Just as He told the woman with chronic bleeding, "go in peace," He welcomed this humble and grateful woman, this sinful and disgraced woman, into His fellowship by these words, and then sent her away with a blessing. By His kind response, He elevated the status of this social outcast, using her as an example of repentant and grateful worship.

The Outcome

What did this woman's life look like after her encounter with Jesus? She was free! Forgiven! Life would never be the same for her, as she experienced a new beginning. She was a transformed person, no longer burdened with guilt and condemnation, but confident of her standing in the eyes of God.

Jesus' forgiveness (for past, present and future sins) would radically change her life and most likely she would become one of His followers in response to the mercy she was shown. This woman could testify that Jesus loved her unconditionally and there are no faults or mistakes (no matter how bad or horrible) that are too far from His gracious touch.

Although her reputation may always have been tainted, no longer did she feel the weight of shame from her past. Jesus' public comments had restored her status in His eyes and that was all that mattered. She would embark along a new path and over time this purity of heart that reflected repentance and gratitude would translate to a purified life, now lovingly walking in the direction of God's will.

"I TELL YOU, THERE IS REJOICING IN THE PRESENCE OF THE ANGELS OF GOD OVER ONE SINNER WHO REPENTS."

Luke 15:10 NIV

A Lesson About Priorities

As Jesus and His disciples were on their way, He entered a village, and a woman named Martha welcomed Him into her home. She had a sister named Mary, who sat at the Lord's feet and was listening to what He said. But Martha was distracted by all the preparations that had to be made. Finally, she went to Jesus and asked, "Lord, don't You care that my sister has left me to do all the work by myself? Tell her to come and help me!"

"Martha, Martha," the Lord answered, "you are worried and upset about so many things, but only one thing is necessary. Mary has chosen what is better and it will not be taken away from her."

ONE THING IS NECESSARY.

Luke 10:38-42

31

THE SCENE

Oh, there was so much preparation to take place prior to the dinner that evening! And this would be no ordinary dinner, as many additional guests were expected because word of Jesus' visit had spread throughout the town. Martha was concerned that she would not be ready for the festivities to begin in a few hours. The arrival of Jesus always brought excitement, but the responsibility for the meal and welcoming the guests fell on Martha's shoulders because she had opened up her home for the gathering. Jesus was a special and honored guest, and she wanted to make sure all the details of His visit were arranged and that the company enjoyed themselves. Martha took her role of hostess seriously and was well-known for being diligent, conscientious and efficient, rarely sitting or resting from all of her household duties.

After greeting Jesus and His disciples at the door, Martha led them to the courtyard to relax prior to the meal. Her sister Mary was also excited that Jesus had arrived and sat down where she could hear every word that He spoke.

Martha looked outside the kitchen area where Jesus and the disciples had congregated. She could see that her sister Mary was sitting at His feet listening intently to His words. Just when Martha had needed her sister's assistance, Mary joined Jesus in conversation. "Doesn't she understand how much I need her to help me?" Martha muttered to herself. Part of her wanted to be with the others as they conversed with Jesus, but she felt responsible for the upcoming meal and there simply was no time to spare.

Martha tried to get Mary's attention and motion for her to come to the kitchen. However, Mary was focused on Jesus and unaware of Martha's growing irritation. With each glance at Mary, Martha's frustration increased. She assumed that it would not seem inappropriate for her to ask Jesus to direct Mary to help her. After all, women were the ones responsible for making and serving the meal, and she needed support if this evening were to be a success. Jesus would certainly understand her request.

Finally, unable to remain silent any longer, Martha approached Jesus and indignantly blurted out, "Lord, don't You care that my sister has left me to do the work by myself? Tell her to come and help me!"

Jesus Looked into Her Heart

Jesus glanced up to meet the glare of Martha and heard her request. He had been watching her bustle within the house making preparations and was not surprised by her outburst. Martha was His friend and had served Him on several occasions because she had a servant's heart and gift for hospitality.

But Martha's tendency toward worrying about the details of the household, though admirable, had created a driven, efficient and somewhat controlling woman whose identity was wrapped up in her reputation as an expert hostess. Martha was never finished with her chores and seemed to be a perfectionist who was continually able to find additional tasks to perform in her household. One look through her eyes, Jesus could see how perturbed and annoyed she was with her sister who had chosen to spend time with Him rather than with the serving duties. Martha was no longer serving with a compassionate heart, but with an agitated one. She was weary and burdened, but seemingly could not afford to take time to rest.

Only Jesus could truly identify the deeper issues that were the source of Martha's irritation. Maybe Martha was judging her sister to be less diligent according to society's expectations of women's roles within the household. Or she could have been feeling overwhelmed by the seemingly endless tasks she was responsible for. Martha was not able to acknowledge Mary's student heart, and it seemed the focus of her concern was more out of frustration that she was bearing the load of the work, rather than disappointment that she was unable to sit at Jesus' feet, too. Though she wouldn't admit it, Martha may have been jealous of her sister.

Looking into Martha's heart, Jesus could see a woman trying to find fulfillment in serving others, but empty from neglecting the true source of fulfillment — time with Him. He knew her fulfillment in this physical life would never be complete, but would come through "resting in Him," sitting at His feet and gaining the spiritual nourishment that her burdened heart needed.

It was time for a lesson about priorities.

HIS RESPONSE

"Martha, Martha," He said in a friendly and loving tone, gracefully trying to settle her down while overlooking her judgmental and demanding attitude. She was "worried and upset" about many things. As the guest and recipient of her hospitality, His tone seemed to communicate His understanding of her tendency to become consumed with her "to-do list," yet He wanted to relieve her from the expectations to be the "perfect hostess" and help her understand how life should be prioritized.

Jesus would also be concerned with the distractions and irritations that caused Martha to make demands of Him and lash out at her sister. Martha's gift of serving was tainted if done with a judgmental attitude or with words of bitterness or self-pity.

"There is only one thing that is necessary and Mary has chosen the right thing," Jesus added, validating the choice her sister had made. His statement that Mary had made the better choice raised the status of women by validating their desire to pursue spiritual matters as students of Jesus, rather than exclusively playing the expected servant role. Jesus would break with societal tradition by encouraging women to focus on spiritual matters by allowing them to share in conversations typically reserved for men. Though life's responsibilities would still remain, the value of women increased as Jesus made a statement regarding the equality of access to Jesus and spiritual teaching.

Even though Jesus was the recipient of Martha's serving heart, He was telling her that it was more important to spend time with the eternal things than get overly wrought about physical things, such as meal preparation. Jesus did not seem to discourage service, in itself, but cautioned Martha not to allow the busyness, even if done in service to Him, to affect her priorities. Worldly pursuits are temporal, whereas spiritual pursuits have eternal consequences.

Jesus would have preferred for Martha to be sitting at His feet, as well, rather than being consumed by the busyness of serving Him. He would have preferred her presence, her heart for Him, and her time with Him. In essence, Jesus gave her permission to simplify and prioritize her life so that she too, would seek the one thing that is necessary, or essential — sitting at the Lord's feet, listening to Him, enjoying His company, sharing life's adventures — experiencing Him!

Jesus may have also implied that Martha had become obsessed with additional details of serving — even frivolous ones. Maybe she was busy with trivial tasks and chores that, if analyzed, could be jettisoned for the more important time of being in worship at Jesus' feet and listening to His words.

By Jesus' response, He reminded Martha not to neglect the relationship — the desire for growing closer to Him — as there is no substitute, not even with the good works of serving. Perhaps Martha wrapped her identity in being a doer, but her identity and true fulfillment would come from time with Jesus.

THE OUTCOME

Later in Scripture, we find Martha serving Jesus again, so it was not the serving itself that Jesus was addressing. Jesus exposed the heart of the issue — the busyness and emotional comparisons that caused Martha to be worried and upset, as well as crowding out time to be with Him. Jesus had given Martha permission to prioritize her relationship with Him. Her household work would always be there — and would get done. But first, she was reminded to arrange to find time to sit at Jesus' feet and learn from Him, as Mary did. He encouraged her to "rest in Him," as she was weary from carrying many burdens.

Martha learned that her identity should be based in Jesus, not in her achievements, efficiency or reputation. Jesus gave her value and worth from being with Him. This value was not based on secular standards of the world, but from eternal values that will not fade away.

Maybe after the conversation, with her priorities straight and realization of her need to have her identity in Jesus, Martha timed her serving and used it as a gift for compassionately serving others, not as a means of defining who she was. Jesus had taught her that even servants can lose focus on the bigger picture, so she would find time to rise above the busyness of the everyday to focus on eternity.

Hopefully, Martha relinquished some of her perfectionist tendencies in order to allow time to sit at Jesus' feet with His other disciples. She continued to serve, but perhaps she moderated her tendency to be consumed and overwhelmed with her "to-do list" and concentrated on her heart-to-heart intimacy with Jesus. She learned that Jesus desired to walk with her — as she focused on Him rather than rushing off to do something for Him. He was more interested in their relationship than on her performance.

And in the process of walking with Jesus, perhaps the underlying emotional reasons for causing Martha to be "worried and upset" were addressed. Underlying irritants were exposed and an apology to her sister restored their relationship.

The lesson of priorities pierced Martha's heart when she heard of Jesus' death. Every moment spent with Him was precious; every word He had spoken burned in her heart. Though the meals she provided had faded away, the relationship with her Lord would remain forever. She had learned that Jesus was central to her life, out of which all of her activities, including service to others, flowed.

"BUT SEEK FIRST THE KINGDOM OF GOD AND HIS RIGHTEOUSNESS, AND ALL THESE THINGS WILL BE PROVIDED FOR YOU."

Matthew 6:33 HCSB

THE DELIVERANCE OF A CRIPPLED WOMAN

Jesus was teaching in one of the synagogues on a Sabbath. A woman was there who had been crippled by an evil spirit for eighteen years. She was completely bent over and could not straighten up at all. When Jesus saw the woman, He called her forward and said to her, "Woman, you are set free from your disability." Then He placed His hands on her, and immediately she straightened up and began to glorify God.

But the synagogue ruler, indignant because Jesus had healed on the Sabbath, responded by telling the crowd, "Each week has six days when work should be done. So come and be healed on one of those days, not on the Sabbath."

The Lord answered him, "You hypocrites! Doesn't each one of you untie your ox or donkey from the feeding trough on the Sabbath and lead it to water? Satan has bound this woman, a daughter of Abraham, for eighteen long years. Shouldn't she be set free from this bondage on the Sabbath day?"

When He had said these things, all His adversaries were humiliated, but the whole crowd was rejoicing over all the glorious things He was doing.

YOU
ARE SET
FREE.

LUKE 13:10-17

THE SCENE

Jesus was in town! A woman heard He was teaching in the synagogue, so she got up early on Sabbath morning to allow extra time for the journey. Though controversy seemed to follow Him, she wondered if Jesus could possibly be the prophesied Messiah. You see, for a woman who had been crippled by an evil spirit, the Messiah was her only hope. Though she had lived with physical limitations for eighteen years, it was hearing the Scriptures read in the synagogue that took her mind off her ever-present pain and hopeless circumstances.

The evil spirit tormented her emotionally, as well, and most likely she battled depression and discouragement. Though it was difficult to make the trek from her home, she attended the synagogue regularly for comfort, inspiration and peace. She found respite for her troubled soul by listening to the Scriptures. Maybe one of her favorites was Isaiah 58:8 that spoke of a time when healing would quickly appear or Zephaniah 3:19 that promised God's rescue of the lame.

Like so many individuals with a disability or deformity, she lived day-to-day quietly resigned to her situation, with no expectation of relief. With each passing year her body deteriorated, the pain increased and mobility decreased. Her muscles seemed frozen in a position that was bent at the waist and she was unable to straighten up. Walking was tedious. She used canes for stability and to periodically lean on for rest. Even daily activities, like preparing a meal, took extra time and were exhausting. Sadly, many years had passed since she was able to participate completely in her family's activities. Oh, how she longed to pick up a child again!

Today she had tried to leave her home earlier than usual so she could find a place toward the front of the synagogue. But that morning was particularly difficult because of the stabbing pain in her back. She considered staying home, but desperately wanted to hear Jesus teach. There was something special about the Teacher called Jesus. Maybe He would bring the deliverance she had prayed for!

As she shuffled along to the synagogue, passersby would glance at her and then quickly look away. Over the years she had become accustomed to being invisible. Though she told herself it did not matter, her heart was familiar with the pain of feeling insignificant.

By the time she arrived, the synagogue was full and the voice of one teaching beckoned her inside. There was something unique about the tone of His voice. Being severely crippled, it was difficult to look up, but she lifted her head with all the strength she could muster. She desperately wanted to see His face because He spoke with such strength and compassion. She was grateful that people opened up a path and she moved toward the front.

What was that? Why were people looking at her? The crowd seemed to part, leaving an open pathway to the Teacher. Was He speaking to her? Yes! She heard the question again, more clearly this time. He was asking her to come forward, to come to Him! He had singled her out! Confused, she moved toward Him and strained all the more to look into His face. Their eyes briefly met before she had to drop her head to relieve the ache in her neck.

Jesus Looked into Her Heart

While Jesus was teaching, He had been aware of the shifting audience making a path for someone progressing toward the front. Turning His head, He saw a woman bended over two stabilizing canes. It took Him one look to assess her condition. Though the crippling of her body was obvious to all, only He had the ability to determine the severity of the spirit that had bound her.

In an instant He understood the depth of her multifaceted suffering. His empathy for this woman motivated Him to act. He understood the full range of emotions that accompany a physical disability and He yearned to give her rest by releasing her from the bondage she had endured for so long.

His Response

Jesus stepped toward her. With the words, "Woman, you are set free!" and the touch of His hands, she stood upright for the first time in eighteen years.

Her canes dropped to the floor. She straightened up her body, raised her arms into the air and proclaimed, "I'm free! Praise God, I'm free!" She was unaware of the scowl on the face of the synagogue ruler because she was absorbed by the impact of this miraculous event. Spontaneously she knelt down in reverence, then sprang up and grasped the hands of Jesus. Looking up into His eyes, she would always remember the look on His face. His wide grin conveyed an expression of radiant joy that she had never seen before. After giving Him a grateful hug, her feet could not contain themselves and she danced several steps with Him.

She heard the synagogue ruler begin to speak, so she backed away from Jesus, continuing to glorify God. The synagogue ruler was indignant that Jesus had healed on the Sabbath. "Hypocrites!" Jesus proclaimed. Shouldn't this woman, a daughter of Abraham, be loosed from the bondage that Satan had imposed for "eighteen long years?" Had He previously seen her in the community and waited for this precise time to heal her, underscoring the supremacy of love as fulfillment of the intent of the Law? Did this statement also demonstrate His divine ability to know at every moment all the details of our lives?

Regardless of the specifics that we are not aware of, Jesus' response was in keeping with His compassionate character. Jesus was undeniably pleased to liberate this woman from the evil spirit that had kept her in physical and emotional bondage for too many years. This woman who was made in God's own image was valued and beautiful in God's eyes. There should be no waiting to relieve a person from suffering. Jesus had said, "Come to Me, all of you who are weary and burdened, and I will give you rest" (Matthew 11:28 HCSB). What better way to demonstrate the intent of the Sabbath rest than to give this woman rest from her suffering!

THE OUTCOME

This woman undoubtedly lived the rest of her days in amazement of the long-awaited deliverance that came through the actions of Jesus. She would never forget the moment when Jesus put His hands on her and she felt a surge of energy and vitality flow through her body. I would imagine her expression of gratitude was uncontainable. She not only continued to glorify God in the synagogue but also praised God while sharing the story of this miracle with all she met.

Though the news of Jesus' trial and death could have been confusing to her, maybe she understood the fulfillment of prophetic Scripture in a deeper way after His resurrection. She would have a personal understanding of the love of God who would send His Son to save His people and demonstrate the full intent of the Law.

As this blessed woman heard Scriptures read in the synagogue she probably listened to them with a new perspective. Her favorite verses had been personally fulfilled in her life, and the Messiah truly had come. Jesus, the Messiah, her Messiah, had come so that she could not only have spiritual life, but be able to live physically and emotionally to the fullest extent. What He had read from the book of Isaiah was true! "The Spirit of the Lord is on Me, because He has anointed Me to preach good news to the poor. He has sent Me to proclaim freedom to the captives and recovery of sight to the blind, to set free the oppressed . . ." (Luke 4:18 HCSB).

Every morning upon awakening she would consciously stretch her newly-straightened back toward the ceiling and relive that moment when Jesus set her free. This woman, a walking miracle who experienced the power of the Son of God, could show undeniable visible proof of being touched by Jesus!

"I HAVE COME THAT THEY MAY HAVE LIFE, AND HAVE IT
TO THE FULL."

John 10:10 NIV

A Mother's Plea

Leaving that place, Jesus withdrew to the region of Tyre and Sidon. He entered a house and did not want anyone to know it, but He could not escape notice. Instead, immediately after hearing about Him, a Canaanite woman from that region whose little daughter was possessed by an evil spirit came out shouting, "Lord, son of David, have mercy on me! My daughter is suffering terribly from demon-possession."

Jesus did not say a word to her. But the woman kept following along and shouting, so His disciples approached Him and urged Him, "Send her away, for she keeps crying out after us." He answered, "I was sent only to the people of Israel! They are like a flock of lost sheep."

LET YOUR DESIRE BE GRANTED.

But the woman came and fell at His feet and begged, "Please help me, Lord!" Jesus replied, "First let the children eat all they want, for it is not right to take the children's bread and toss it to their dogs."

"Lord, that's true," the woman said, "but even the dogs eat the crumbs that fall from their masters' table."

Jesus answered, "Woman, you have great faith! Your request is granted. Because of this reply, you may go. The demon has left your daughter." Her daughter was healed from that very hour. She went home and found her child lying on the bed, and the demon gone.

MATTHEW 15:21-28
MARK 7:24-30

THE SCENE

Word of Jesus' power to cast out demons traveled quickly from town to town and reached a woman with a daughter who was suffering intolerably at the hand of a demon, an evil spirit. The moment she heard of this man, she determined to seek Him out, no matter the cost. She knew that Jesus was Jewish and risked being rebuffed not only because of her Gentile heritage, being an "outsider," but additionally because she was a woman. But she needed to find Him!

There is a special connection between a mother and her child. Because of that intense bond, this woman was considerably distressed to witness her daughter's agony. Nothing could be done to relieve the suffering caused by the demon. No relief was permanent, and watching the torment of her precious child was more than she could bear. Nothing was more important than to see the health of her child restored, to see her daughter once again playing happily with other children and living life as intended.

Doctors could not cure her daughter's ailment. This was a spiritual condition that she recognized could only be healed with spiritual power. The numerous accounts of Jesus' miracles were convincing. She believed that Jesus was the person who could heal her daughter. But would He help a Canaanite? And a woman, no less?

She found Jesus and began to follow Him, calling out to Him and begging Him to heal her daughter. There was no response. Out of desperation, she persisted by crying out for His attention, receiving only disdainful glances from those accompanying Him. She had nothing to lose — the only option that remained at home was the presence of an evil spirit in her child and the disgrace of being treated as social outcasts — so she continued to pursue Him. Frustrated with her insistent pleading and her incessant calls for mercy, Jesus' disciples urged Him to send her away.

Walking on, Jesus spoke to His disciples, as if ignoring her pleas. He reminded them that He was sent to the lost sheep of the house of Israel, implying that Gentiles were not the focus of His ministry. She overheard His comment but respectfully persisted, falling at His feet. "Lord, please help me!" Jesus turned and faced a woman kneeling with uplifted hands.

Jesus Looked into Her Heart

Jesus looked down to see a mother's face, strained with concern and fear over the plight of her daughter. Tear-filled eyes conveyed the depth of her distressed heart, worried only for the welfare of her child. This woman was willing to do whatever was necessary to pursue the man who she perceived was able to provide the healing relief her little child so desperately needed. This mother was not ashamed or too proud to kneel before Jesus, to beg for help and mercy on behalf of her child.

Jesus understood why a mother would risk her reputation and defy cultural standards to beg for help. He recognized the attachment that is created and solidified during a period of nine months when a woman is aware of a baby — her own child — developing inside her womb. That natural motherly bond deepens while holding her newborn to her breast and through the process of caring for her helpless, totally dependent baby.

For a mother, there is nothing more debilitating than to watch her child suffer. Perhaps for an instant, Jesus realized that in the not too distant future He would be staring into the face of another mother, His own, as she would agonize while watching her own grown child suffer. Yes, He understood.

Jesus gazed at the face of a humble woman. Humble, yet etched with uncommon determination in petitioning Him, even when ignored by Him and rebuked by those accompanying Him. As Jesus looked into her heart, He perceived a woman whose strong will conveyed trust and faith in His ability to heal and deliver her daughter from a life of despair and torment. She believed in the stories about His acts of mercy that had spread to her small town, and she trusted Him completely to extend His reputation of mercy and love to her child.

HIS RESPONSE

Jesus' initial response to her request for intervention implied that she was outside His sphere of ministry. He said it wasn't right to take the food from the children of priority, the house of Israel, and give it to their pet dogs. Though the term "dog" could have been taken with offense, she remained undeterred. She maintained her composure and prepared her rebuttal. She did not give up, but pressed on with a plea of mercy in the form of a respectful argument.

Her reply was tactful, persistent and bold. She was resolute in requesting any assistance from the One she believed could heal, even if that would include "leftovers that fall from the table." She was aware that her status as a Gentile and a woman could have been outside of Jesus' purpose and circle of influence, but she would be grateful for even a few crumbs, not demanding or expecting anything.

It was this polite statement, conveying her faith, which elicited the answer she diligently sought. Jesus commended this Canaanite woman for her great faith and compassionately granted her heartfelt desire. Her child was instantly healed, just as she trusted would happen. Although she remains nameless in the Biblical account of her story, Jesus knew this woman's name and included her and her daughter in an eternal relationship with Him.

THE OUTCOME

After returning home, this meek, yet courageous woman found her daughter restored to health. Though not by her bedside, Jesus had healed her daughter by speaking His will. Undoubtedly, this mother would tell all who were aware of her child's condition about her conversation with Jesus and His merciful response. Surely the story would be recounted through the years, as she watched her daughter grow stronger and more beautiful, living free from suffering.

Is it possible that as she told her friends and family about her encounter with Jesus the stage was set for their foundational belief when news of His eventual death and resurrection reached their village? Would she recognize this man who she called "Son of David" as the prophesied Messiah? Would others recognize Him by remembering the story of this miracle? Maybe God would use the story of this mother — humble, tenacious and faith-filled — to bring many to believe in Jesus as Savior of all.

"Ask and it will be given to you; seek and you will find; knock and the door will be opened to you."

Matthew 7:7 NIV

A Widow's Two Small Coins

Jesus sat down opposite the temple treasury and watched how the crowd dropped money into the offering box. He looked up and saw some rich people dropping their gifts into the offering box. Many rich people threw in large amounts. He also saw a poor widow put in two very small coins, worth only a fraction of a penny.

She Has Given All She Had.

Summoning His disciples, Jesus said, "I tell you the truth, this poor widow has put more into the treasury than all the others. Everyone else gave out of their surplus, but she, out of her poverty, has put in everything — all she had to live on."

Mark 12:41-44
Luke 21:1-4

THE SCENE

Life had not been kind to her. Widowed, with no inheritance or children to support her, she faced each day as it came. This lonely woman missed her husband dearly, and though she longed for a family of her own, she was thankful that God had treated her with favor and provided for her daily needs. She knew it was by His hand that a family recently asked her to assist them with their household chores in exchange for a modest wage. After calculating that the amount earned would barely cover daily food and rent for her small living area, she praised God for His generosity towards her.

Today was special because she received not one, but two coins for finishing the family's pile of mending. After giving her employer a grateful hug, she departed their house and decided to visit the Temple on her way home. She found great peace when visiting the Temple and decided to linger today in thoughtful prayer. Firmly planted in her heart was faith that a Messiah would come with deliverance for those who were poor and oppressed. Oh, how she longed for such a time!

Surprisingly, a larger crowd than usual was milling around the grounds. She pressed towards the treasury, weaving quietly between worshippers. At times there was quite a bit of fanfare around the area where people came to place their monetary gifts into the offering box. Occasionally, an announcement was made as to the amount that an individual had deposited. She smiled to herself. Certainly no proclamation would be made about her offering. In fact, it was almost laughable to think that the two coins in her pocket had any significance at all.

But she had already determined to give the two small coins as an offering because of God's faithfulness towards her. Pulling the coins out of her pocket, she whispered a prayer of gratitude and dropped them in the box. She stepped away, casually looked up and caught a brief glimpse of a man seated across the way who was smiling at her. His kind look was in stark contrast to the condescending glances given when depositing her paltry contribution. Humbly, she lowered her eyes and quickly continued on her way.

JESUS LOOKED INTO HER HEART

Jesus and His disciples had been watching the parade of people deposit their money into the offering boxes when this woman caught His attention. What a study in contrasts! Her faded and frayed dress looked even plainer next to the fine robes of the wealthy. Additionally, her unassuming demeanor was noticeably different than those who looked self-assured about the large sums of money they had just contributed.

But it was the look in her eyes that made the loudest statement. Her unpretentious countenance reflected the pure heart of a woman who understood her status from God's perspective. Though she had lost the worldly worth of the status and financial security of a married woman, she understood the true value of life and had found contentment in widowhood. God was everything to her, and all she had left to give was her life. This woman's assurance of hope in her eternal reward translated through her serene eyes, and it made Jesus smile.

Never losing any opportunity to teach His disciples, Jesus called them closer, gesturing toward the woman He had been observing. Most likely she did not hear Jesus' words, as His response was directed to the disciples.

HIS RESPONSE

"I tell you the truth that this poor widow has put more into the offering box than all the others." Quizzical expressions came across the disciples faces. All could see that she had only given two small coins, while many rich people were throwing in large sums.

Jesus continued, "For all of them gave out of their wealth, what they could easily spare. But she, out of her poverty, has given all she had to live on." He not only acknowledged her generosity but addressed society's standard of a person's worth. It was commonly thought that the wealthy were more favored in God's eyes, but Jesus continually put all of God's children on equal footing.

Though she was a woman, poor and a widow (all categories of low status in her society), Jesus made it clear that she did not have lesser value to God. She was not insignificant. In fact, by her example of sacrificial giving and sincere motives, He elevated her status, affirming the value of a pure heart.

Jesus did not condemn the rich for giving out of wealth, but emphasized the worth of one who society judged as "worthless." This woman had a heart of gold and that is what mattered. Though already poor, she still gave, not holding back anything. From a human perspective, her offering paled in comparison. But Jesus made the point that God is aware of even the smallest gift. No act of giving, and more importantly, no person goes unnoticed.

THE OUTCOME

This woman's situation did not change after this non-verbal encounter with Jesus. In fact, she was probably unaware that Jesus' comments were even made about her. She might have been embarrassed to know her example of generosity would inspire millions throughout the centuries. But she would have been pleased with Jesus' affirmation that those who are devalued, overlooked and marginalized have value in the eyes of God.

Just as with this poor widow, there may be times when you sense that humans do not value you and your life seems insignificant and useless. Maybe you are not rich, famous, beautiful, specially gifted or have societal status. But do you sense Jesus' loving glance as you humbly come to Him? As you give of yourself, even your entire life, are you assured of validation in Jesus' eyes, giving you contentment and peace? Just as this poor widow understood the true meaning of life, do you believe that temporal values will pass away? Do you place your hope in the eternal? In Jesus' eyes, you are noticed, significant, valued and loved!

"BLESSED ARE THE PURE IN HEART, FOR THEY WILL SEE GOD."

Matthew 5:8 NIV

A Woman Fully Known

Now He had to travel through Samaria, so He came to the town called Sychar. It was near the field that Jacob had long ago given to his son Joseph. Jacob's well was still there, and Jesus, worn out from His journey, sat down at the well.

It was noon, and after Jesus' disciples had gone into town to buy some food, a Samaritan woman came to draw some water from the well. Jesus said to her, "Will you give Me a drink of water?" The Samaritan woman said to Him, "You are a Jew and I am a Samaritan woman. How can You ask me for a drink?" (For Jews do not associate with Samaritans.)

Jesus answered her, "If you knew the gift of God, that is who it is that asks you for a drink, you would ask Him and He would give you living water."

"Sir," the woman said, "You don't even have a bucket and the well is deep. So where do you get this 'living water'? You aren't greater than our father Jacob, are you? He gave us the well and drank from it himself, as did his sons and livestock."

Jesus answered, "Everyone who drinks this water will get thirsty again. But whoever drinks the water I give him will never be thirsty again — ever! Indeed, the water I give him will become a spring of water inside him welling up to eternal life."

"Sir," the woman said to Him, "give me this water so that I won't get thirsty and have to keep coming here to draw water." He told her, "Go, call your husband and come back." "I have no husband," she replied.

Jesus said to her, "You're right when you say you have no husband! For you've had five husbands and the man you are now living with isn't your husband! What you have said is true." "Sir," the woman replied, "I can see that You are a prophet. Our fathers worshiped on this mountain, but you Jews claim that the place where we must worship is in Jerusalem."

Jesus declared, "Believe me, woman, the time is coming when you will worship the Father neither on this mountain nor in Jerusalem. You Samaritans worship what you do not know. We worship what we do know, because salvation is from the Jews. But a time is coming and has now come when the true worshipers will worship the Father in spirit and truth for they're the kind of worshipers the Father seeks. God is Spirit, and those who worship God must be led by the Spirit to worship Him according to the truth."

The woman said, "I know that the Messiah will come. He is the one we call Christ. When He comes, He will explain everything to us." Then Jesus declared, "I am [He], the One speaking to you."

Just then His disciples arrived, and they were amazed that He was talking with a woman. But none of them asked, "What do You want?" or "Why are You talking with her?"

Then the woman left her water jar, went back to the town and said to the people, "Come, see a man who told me everything I have ever done. Could this be the Messiah?" They left the town and made their way toward Him. Many of the Samaritans from that town believed in Him because of the woman's testimony, "He told me everything I ever did." They urged Him to stay with them, and He stayed two more days. Many more Samaritans put their faith in Jesus because of what He said. They told the woman, "We no longer believe just because of what you said; now we have heard for ourselves, and we are certain that this man really is the Savior of the world."

I AM HE.

JOHN 4:4-30, 39-42

THE SCENE

Here she was again — going through her typical routine of walking to Jacob's well to draw water. Most women arranged their trips to the well during the cool of the day, but facing the other town women was awkward. She avoided them by making her trek in the middle of the day.

The nagging ache in her heart would not go away. Life certainly had not turned out as she expected or planned. No one seemed to understand her unsettled heart and discontentment. Certainly her actions towards the town men did not help her cause. She was embarrassed to admit that she used her beauty to attract a man and yes, she was difficult to live with. It didn't take long for the man to leave, confirming her worthlessness and deepening her loneliness. The cycle would repeat again. This was all she could trust.

How she longed for a friend — someone to talk to who understood her and would not judge her because of her failings. She felt so hollow at times. The men in her life did not fill the hole in her heart. With each failed relationship her reputation as a desperate and desolate woman was solidified. Life was confusing and meaningless.

Women shunned her, and men took advantage of her emotional weakness. Here she was again on yet another scorching ordinary day, wishing for a fresh start or a way to undo the grief and heartache she had caused. If she could run away . . . well, she just could not bear to face anyone today.

Oh, groan, there was someone sitting by the well. A man. She certainly did not feel charming today. A Jewish man. He definitely would not speak to her, a Samaritan woman. Avoiding His glance, she quickly proceeded to draw water into her empty jar. Wiping the sweat from her brow, she poured water into a cup and began to take a drink.

"Please give me a drink of water." What?! She couldn't believe that this Jewish man had actually spoken to her and she looked up.

Jesus Looked Into Her Heart

Jesus was exhausted from His travels and had stopped at Jacob's well for a drink. Even though there was great animosity between the Jews and Samaritans, Jesus chose to pass through Samaria. While resting, He watched a Samaritan woman approach. At first glance, she was an average woman going about her daily routine. But there was something unusual about this woman. She was all alone in the heat of the day, and Jesus could see that she was deep in thought and avoiding eye contact with Him.

After His request for a drink of water, she was now looking directly at Him with a look of astonishment on her face. With a skeptical tone she replied, "How can You ask me for a drink? You are a Jew and I am a Samaritan woman." Maybe she was slightly annoyed that yet again, a man was asking for something from her. But the tone of this man's request and the way He looked at her was different. Her guard was down, the mask was off and the dialogue was about to begin.

Looking through her cautious eyes, Jesus could see a restless woman who made no attempt to conceal her dissatisfied and empty heart. She was thirsty, but not necessarily for water. She was thirsty for Life, and He was the only One who could fill her dry and weary soul.

HIS RESPONSE

With a unique twist of the conversation, Jesus said that if she knew God's gift, that is Who was asking for a drink, then she would have asked Him and He would have given her living water. She was intrigued about this living water and asked Him to give her this water so she would not get thirsty and have to keep coming back for more. Jesus had her attention and now told her, "Go, call your husband and come back." He knew this was her heart's soft spot — that of unfulfilled love and loss. Relationally, she was continually thirsty, but never satisfied.

With downcast eyes she quietly replied, "I have no husband." Without hesitation, He confirmed that she was right. "You've had five husbands and you're not married to the man you're living with now!" She was shocked! How could He have known about her personal life? Who was this man?

"Sir, I can see that You are a prophet." She changed the subject to that of religion, contrasting where the Samaritans and "you people," the Jews, worship. But Jesus pointed out that there was a time coming — actually it was there now — when true believers will be led by the Spirit to worship in truth, hinting that God was reconciling both groups, the Samaritans and Jews, and making Himself accessible to all.

Her face brightened and with deep conviction of expressed hope the woman stated, "I know that Messiah is coming, and when He comes, He will tell us everything." All the unanswered questions she had about life would be explained when the Messiah she longed for came.

"I, the person speaking to you, am He." Jesus said it! He chose to reveal Himself as Messiah to this outcast Gentile woman. Momentarily, her face was frozen in an expression of awe, wonder and puzzlement. When the disciples arrived, they were surprised to find Jesus talking with a woman, but did not interrupt to question Him because they could sense the intimacy of the conversation. Though we are not privy to the remaining dialogue, the effect of Jesus' encounter with this Samaritan woman was profound.

THE OUTCOME

Suddenly, trivial matters, such as drawing water were unimportant. Leaving her water jar behind, she hurried back to town to share what had just happened. "Come and see a man who told me everything I have ever done! Could it be that this is the Messiah?" His ability to look into her heart and fully understand her life convinced her that this man could be the Anointed One, the Christ! Jesus Himself even declared that He was the One!

Jesus had miraculously opened her eyes to see that He alone had the answers to her questions and simultaneously provided the solution to her misdirected longings. Previously, her quest to understand the mysteries of life had sent her down a path that left her feeling shallow and unfulfilled. But one encounter with Jesus transformed her. Life was no longer meaningless. She now had new perspective — an eternal perspective.

What was so persuasive about this woman's story that influenced the town people to make their way toward Jesus? Maybe it was because her countenance had changed. Her eyes danced with joy and a smile filled her face! Surprisingly, there was new passion in her voice. The issues that had consumed her were no longer of concern. She was settled and her heart was overflowing with joy. She was whole, restored and fully alive! Life had clarity. This marginalized woman was suddenly different, and the people were intrigued by this remarkable transformation. So out of curiosity, they came to see the man she was so excited about.

The encounter with the woman at the well revealed that Jesus, the Messiah, is the One who gives living water and eternal life. The Samaritan woman persuasively told others this good news about Jesus, encouraging them to "come and see" for themselves.

And because of one woman sharing her personal experience, many of the Samaritans also believed He was the Messiah, the one called Christ, the Savior of the world.

"IF ANYONE IS THIRSTY, HE SHOULD COME TO ME AND DRINK! THE ONE WHO BELIEVES IN ME, AS THE SCRIPTURE HAS SAID, WILL HAVE STREAMS OF LIVING WATER FLOW FROM DEEP WITHIN HIM."

John 7:37-38 HCSB

A MERCIFUL RESCUE

At dawn He appeared again in the temple courts, and all the people were coming to Him. He sat down and began to teach them. The teachers of the law and the Pharisees brought in a woman who had been caught in bed with a man who wasn't her husband. They made her stand in the middle of the crowd and said to Jesus, "Teacher, this woman was caught in the act of committing adultery. The Law of Moses teaches that a woman like this should be stoned to death. So what do You say?" They asked this to trap Him, in order that they might have evidence to accuse Him.

But Jesus bent down and started writing on the ground with His finger. When they persisted in questioning Him, He stood up and said to them, "If any one of you is without sin, let him be the first to throw a stone at her." Then He stooped down again and continued writing on the ground.

When they heard this, they left, one by one, starting with the older men, until only Jesus was left, with the woman still standing there. Jesus stood up and asked her, "Woman, where are they? Has no one condemned you?"

"No one, Lord," she answered. "Then neither do I condemn you," Jesus declared. "You may go now, but don't sin anymore."

HAS NO ONE CONDEMNED YOU?

JOHN 8:2-11

THE SCENE

With eyes closed, one can almost hear the commotion created as the group of men ran toward Jesus with a disheveled woman in tow. She struggled to maintain her balance as she was pushed by those around her. A crowd was gathering, running alongside to witness the inevitable confrontation. Eager for a quick display of justice, they hurled accusations at her while they hustled toward the Temple. Undoubtedly, Jesus heard the uproar and was aware of the developing scene as they approached His seated position.

Shoving her toward Jesus, they called His name. He looked up to see a frightened woman who was grasping the clothes that had been hurriedly put on after being caught in the act of adultery. Her tear-filled eyes were cast to the ground. The reality of her situation was overwhelming, and she was overcome with humiliation and helplessness. Well aware of the consequences of her sin, she shuddered at the thought of facing the expected judgment.

Trying to disguise their motives, the religious leaders phrased their question to Jesus, "In our Law, Moses commanded that such a woman be stoned to death. What do You say?"

Jesus saw through the veil of their righteous indignation and into their hypocritical and conniving hearts. The accusers had callously exploited this woman by using her as bait to trap Him. They were more concerned with exposing Jesus as a fraud than with her as a person. Their double standard of morality was also apparent as they were quick to charge a woman for adultery, yet her adulterous male partner was nowhere to be seen. In essence, these men could not see that her obvious lack of morality matched their own.

Refraining from looking at those questioning Him, Jesus calmly began writing something in the dirt. The woman was holding her breath, her very life dependent upon His response. The noisy crowd quieted. All were waiting for His answer.

Jesus stood up and gave a penetrating look at each of her accusers. Then He spoke in a commanding, yet gracious tone, "The one of you who is without sin, let him be the first to throw a stone at her." Without another word, Jesus bent down and continued to write in the dust.

This challenging statement delivered a conviction of unconfessed sin. Each person present was forced to recognize not only his own sinfulness, but the possibility that this man might truly be the Son of God. The woman watched with relief as one by one, the men left the scene — an acknowledgement of their own sin. She was left alone with Jesus. "What would He do to her?" she wondered.

Jesus stood up and faced the woman.

JESUS LOOKED INTO HER HEART

Jesus looked into eyes filled with tears that reflected a heart aching from guilt, shame and hopelessness. Only He could perfectly understand the reason why this woman was involved in an illegal relationship. Was she seeking love from someone other than her husband because she was in a marriage that was loveless or abusive? Had she been tossed out of a marriage by a heartless husband without a proper bill of divorcement that allowed her to legally remarry? Did she seek the attention of another man because he provided financial or emotional support? Even within this illicit relationship, had she been exploited for political gain by her lover? Had her emotional vulnerability been used to her partner's advantage?

No matter the reason, Jesus saw standing in front of Him a desperate woman who had lost her way and was living outside of God's will for her life. She was pursuing love and acceptance, but from a relationship other than the one God had originally intended — a marriage that was bound by covenant.

HIS RESPONSE

"Where are they? Has no one condemned you?" In contrast to the harshness she had been previously subjected to, Jesus treated her with dignity. She acknowledged that no man remained.

"Then neither do I condemn you," He replied. "Go and sin no more."

Jesus did not condemn her, but He also did not condone her sinful actions. Instead, He challenged her to a lifestyle change — commanding her to leave her life of sin that would never satisfy her lonely heart. Pursuing an adulterous affair was not God's will for her ultimate happiness. His compassionate act of redemption emphasized that anything outside of God's intent could never bring fulfillment, only guilt and negative consequences.

By His merciful response, this woman had just experienced the psalmist's statement, "He will not always accuse . . . He does not treat us as our sins deserve" (Psalm 103:9-10 NIV).

THE OUTCOME

What relief! She didn't immediately rush away, but lingered, taking in the reality of her situation. Who was this man who had rescued her? There was something different about Him. Though not condoning her sinful action, He seemed to understand her plight as a woman. Treated with contempt by other men, Jesus showed her respect. Judged and condemned by other men, Jesus showered her with redemptive mercy and grace.

I wonder how this redeemed woman would have responded. Maybe she was initially too stunned to react. Did she later seek Jesus out to express her thankfulness? Would she watch Jesus from a distance as He taught the masses and eventually become one of His followers? Did their eyes ever meet again? Would she witness the upcoming events when Jesus was subjected to unjust condemnation from a crowd?

What would it have been like for her to be legally condemned by religious leaders seeking justice for a sinful action, and then rescued from imminent execution? Could she sense that Jesus saw her human value and loveliness? This man perceived her lonely heart, accepted her as a person, yet challenged her to live a life of holiness. The impact on her life must have been profound!

Even though her guilt most assuredly was mercifully erased by forgiveness, this woman's situation may not have changed. In fact, she may have faced additional adversity as a consequence of the sin and public disgrace of being an unfaithful wife. Maybe her husband would divorce her. Most likely, this woman's reputation was forever tainted. Would her former accusers retaliate in another way because they were thwarted in their attempt to trap Jesus?

No matter what she endured the rest of her life as a result of sinful choices, undoubtedly she would cherish this encounter with a man who treated her with undeserved compassion and rescued her from punishment, a death sentence. One would hope this woman lived with an acute appreciation of Jesus' loving forgiveness and therefore, carefully and respectfully walked a path that reflected her gratitude for this remarkable act of redemption when guilt and condemnation were released, and she was given a second chance to live untarnished in God's eyes.

"GOD DID NOT SEND HIS SON INTO THE WORLD TO CONDEMN ITS PEOPLE. HE SENT HIM TO SAVE THEM! NO ONE WHO HAS FAITH IN GOD'S SON WILL BE CONDEMNED. BUT EVERYONE WHO DOESN'T HAVE FAITH IN HIM HAS ALREADY BEEN CONDEMNED FOR NOT HAVING FAITH IN GOD'S ONLY SON."

John 3:17-18 CEV

Martha's Belief in the Messiah

A man named Lazarus was sick. He was from Bethany, the village of Mary and her sister Martha. This was the same Mary who later anointed the Lord with fragrant oil and wiped His feet with her hair. The sisters sent a message to Jesus, "Lord, the one You love is sick."

When Jesus heard this, He said, "This sickness will not end in death. No, it is for God's glory so that the Son of God may be glorified through it." Jesus loved Martha and her sister and Lazarus. Yet when He heard that Lazarus was sick, He stayed where He was for two more days. Then He said to the disciples, "Let us go back to Judea."

When Jesus got to Bethany, He found that Lazarus had already been in the tomb four days. Bethany was less than two miles from Jerusalem and many Jews had come to comfort Martha and Mary because their brother had died. When Martha heard that Jesus was coming, she went out to meet Him, but Mary stayed in the house.

Martha said to Jesus, "Lord, if You had been here, my brother would not have died. Yet even now I know that whatever You ask from God, God will give You." Jesus said to her, "Your brother will rise again." Martha answered, "I know that he will rise again in the resurrection at the last day." Jesus said to her, "I am the resurrection and the life! The one who believes in Me will live, even if he dies. Everyone who lives and believes in Me will never die — ever. Do you believe this?" She said to Him, "Yes, Lord, I believe that You are the Messiah, the Son of God, who was to come into the world."

After saying this, she went back and called her sister Mary aside. "The Teacher is here and is asking for you." When Mary heard this, she got up quickly and went to Him. Jesus had not yet entered the village, but was still at the place where Martha had met Him. The Jews who were with her in the house consoling her saw that Mary got up quickly and went out. So they followed her, supposing that she was going to the tomb to mourn there. When Mary came to where Jesus was and saw Him, she fell at His feet and told Him, "Lord, if You had been here, my brother would not have died!"

When Jesus saw her weeping and the Jews who had come along with her also weeping, He was deeply moved in spirit and troubled. "Where have you put his body?" He asked. "Come and see, Lord," they replied. Jesus wept. Then the Jews said, "See how He loved him!" But some of them said, "Couldn't He who opened the blind man's eyes also have kept this man from dying?"

Jesus, once more deeply moved, came to the tomb. It was a cave with a stone rolled against the entrance. "Remove the stone," Jesus said. "But Lord," said Martha, the sister of the dead man, "you know that Lazarus has been dead four days, and there will be a bad smell." Jesus said to her, "Didn't I tell you that if you believed you would see the glory of God?"

So they removed the stone. Then Jesus looked up and said, "Father, I thank You that You have heard Me. I know that You always hear Me. But I said this so that the people here may believe You sent Me." When Jesus finished praying, He shouted, "Lazarus! Come out!"

The man who had been dead came out. His hands and feet were wrapped with strips of linen, and a cloth covered his face. Jesus said to them, "Take off the grave clothes and let him go!" Therefore many of the Jews who had come to visit Mary, and had seen what Jesus did, believed in Him.

I AM THE RESURRECTION AND THE LIFE.

JOHN 11:1-7, 17-45

67

THE SCENE

One of Jesus' friends, Lazarus, suddenly became ill. His sisters, Martha and Mary, were also close friends and had spent numerous hours visiting with Jesus when He was in Bethany. There was no hesitation about sending word to Jesus concerning Lazarus' illness because they had already witnessed His miraculous healing power and assumed that He would immediately return to restore their brother.

But Jesus had other plans. Though He was aware of Lazarus' illness and the distress of His friends, He lingered. He followed the will of His Father, knowing God's glory would be revealed through the events He would orchestrate.

"Where could Jesus be? Why hasn't He responded? Surely He knows how desperately we need Him now!" Martha and Mary struggled to trust Jesus and fought against disappointment, but continued to anticipate His arrival. Lazarus progressively grew weaker. He quickly succumbed and was buried. Martha and Mary were crushed and in shock. Not only had they lost their brother, but now they had doubts about Jesus. Why hadn't He come?

Many friends and family were gathered at Martha's and Mary's house to comfort the sisters. A visitor burst through the door announcing, "Jesus is on His way!" Immediately, Martha wrapped a shawl around her head and hurried out to greet Him. Looking down the path, she searched the faces of those approaching. There He was! Though weary from grief, she brightened with relief when she saw Him.

Rushing toward Him, she blurted out, "Lord, if You had been here, my brother would not have died." Then she respectfully added, "But even now I know that God will give You whatever You ask."

Jesus Looked Into Her Heart

Dear Martha — such a faithful friend. He, along with many others, had been the recipient of her gift of hospitality, as she was well known for her competent ability to organize events. Now, looking through her eyes, He could see the complex mix of emotions — grief and hope, doubt and trust, assertiveness and reliance, impatience and faith, confusion and deference. Jesus loved how her natural tendencies toward management had mellowed after His reminder about priorities. He also knew how difficult it was for her to relinquish control and patiently trust Him.

It deeply moved Jesus to see the pain in Martha's eyes. Lazarus was dead and His cherished friends were overcome with sorrow. Their belief in Jesus had grown during their friendship, but now it was being tested. They could not see beyond their narrow, human viewpoint.

His Response

Jesus gave Martha a comforting embrace and said reassuringly, "Your brother will rise again." Yes, Martha believed that Lazarus would rise again at the Resurrection in the future. In her mind though, that still did not take away her present confusion at Jesus' actions or deep pain from the loss of her brother.

Jesus spoke again, "I am the resurrection and the life! Whoever puts his trust in Me will live, even though he dies; and everyone living and trusting in Me will never die. Do you believe this?"

"Yes, Lord, I believe that You are the Messiah, the Son of God, the One who was to come into the world." Martha's statement of faith affirmed she believed with all of her heart that Jesus was the prophesied Messiah and had the authority to give eternal life. But the reality still remained — Lazarus was dead. Would Jesus do something in this life, or in the one to come?

THE OUTCOME

Martha went back into the house where her distraught sister Mary was being consoled by friends. When Mary was told Jesus was asking to see her, she quickly left the house. When she saw Him, she too told Jesus, "Lord, if You had been here, my brother would not have died." Mary also trusted in His healing power and assumed that had He been there, Lazarus would have been healed. But it was clear Jesus had not come through as both expected.

"Where have you buried him?" Jesus calmly asked. "Come and see," they replied. Then they led Him to the tomb, weeping as they walked. It pained Jesus to see how heartbroken His friends were and how human perspective limited their belief. He too wept. His love for His friends was undeniable to observers, though many also questioned why Jesus allowed Lazarus to die.

What happened next turned the world upside down, not only for those witnessing the event, but for those who would hear the story repeated. When Jesus asked Martha to take away the stone, she resisted, knowing that Lazarus had been dead four days and the body would stink. But Jesus gently reminded her that if she would keep trusting, she would see the glory of God. So the stone to Lazarus' grave was removed and the crowd quieted down, hands placed over their noses in anticipation. No odor! Quizzical looks covered faces, then all eyes turned to Jesus.

Jesus offered up a brief prayer so those present would believe He had been sent by His heavenly Father. Then, with the words "Lazarus, come out!" the unthinkable happened. The man, previously dead for four days, walked out of the tomb with strips of burial linen wrapped around his body. Those in the crowd stared in disbelief, initially stunned into silence. "Unwrap him!" Lazarus was unveiled and then spontaneous and boisterous praise began! Martha and Mary rushed to give Lazarus hugs, their tears of joy flowing freely.

The dramatic intervention in the lives of Jesus' closest friends started the commotion that eventually led to His arrest. He certainly must have known that this display of divine power would unleash a fury of opposition, but He would not have had it any other way, for this was the plan. Jesus chose His friends as the recipients of this blessing and miracle of restored life, and He willingly sacrificed His safety because of His tender love for them. As a result, many would believe He was the Messiah.

Martha had learned to surrender her proclivity to control and arrange her life by completely depending on Jesus, trusting in His power and on His timing. Truly, the timing of this amazing miracle was perfect! Jesus' timing is always perfect, orchestrated to bring glory to His heavenly Father.

One would assume that Martha, Mary and Lazarus would be among the most ardent and vocal witnesses to the divinity of Jesus, as they personally experienced His undeniable power — the power to heal, to restore and to resurrect. They would testify that without a doubt, Jesus is the Resurrection and the Life!

""For this is the will of My Father: that everyone who sees the Son and believes in Him may have eternal life, and I will raise him up on the last day."

John 6:40 HCSB

MARY'S EXPRESSION OF DEVOTION

Six days before the Passover, Jesus came to Bethany, where Lazarus lived, the man whom Jesus had raised from the dead. While Jesus was in Bethany in the home of a man known as Simon the Leper, a dinner was given in Jesus' honor. Martha served, and Lazarus was one of those reclining at the table with Him.

Then Mary came with an alabaster jar filled of pure and expensive fragrant oil of nard. She broke the jar and poured the perfume on Jesus' head as He was reclining at the table. She poured it on Jesus' feet and wiped them with her hair, and the sweet smell of perfume filled the house. When the disciples saw this, they were indignant. "Why this waste of perfume?" they asked. And they rebuked her harshly.

Then one of His disciples, Judas Iscariot, who was about to betray Him, objected, "Why wasn't this perfume sold and the money given to the poor? It was worth a year's wages!" He didn't say this because he cared about the poor but because he was a thief. He was in charge of the money bag and sometimes would steal from it.

SHE HAS DONE A BEAUTIFUL THING FOR ME.

Jesus knew what they were thinking and said to them, "Leave her alone! Why are you bothering this woman? She kept this perfume for the day of My burial. She has done a beautiful thing for Me. You will always have the poor with you, and you can help them any time you want. But you will not always have Me. She has done all she could do; she has anointed My body in advance to prepare it for burial. I tell you the truth, wherever the good news is told in the world, what this woman has done will also be told in memory of her."

MATTHEW 26:6-13
MARK 14:3-9
JOHN 12:1-8

THE SCENE

A dinner in Jesus' honor was held after Lazarus was raised from the dead, and though the religious leaders were known to be actively seeking His arrest, Jesus' friends courageously gathered. Mary was especially excited to see Jesus, as she always looked forward to listening to what He had to say. Honestly, it was more than just listening to His words and teachings — she loved being with Him. She wanted to drink in every nuance of His tone, His thinking and His feelings. She wanted to know Him completely, including His message of life and truth, His purpose — and His heart.

From the moment Mary saw Jesus step through the door, she sensed a change in His demeanor, but she was not quite sure how to describe it. She had witnessed the varied nature of His personality — lighthearted, even playful, serious, joyful and authoritative. Most recently, He had shown the tender empathy of a friend when she was grieving.

Because she had spent so much time studying Jesus, her intuition told her something was different about Him. Was it a heaviness of heart? A foreboding mood? Was He contemplative? It was not sorrow, but was it turmoil? His disposition was not directed inward — it could never be said that Jesus was focused inward. In fact, He seemed to want to linger and be with His friends, clearly enjoying their company.

But Mary sensed that He would be leaving soon. Though she did not completely understand it, there was something unsettling about the nature of His recent messages. Where was He going? Reflecting on His words, random thoughts popped in her head . . . something would be required of Him . . . of her . . . sacrifice, death, resurrection, life. Maybe she was just recalling the amazing events surrounding Lazarus' death and restoration to life. No, there was definitely an ominous feeling at this gathering.

Oh, how she loved this man, this Son of God. But not in a typical human sense. Yes, He was her friend, but so much more. Jesus was her Teacher, Master and Lord. He meant everything to her. She desired to demonstrate her devotion, but how could she possibly express the depths of her heart? Of course — she knew exactly what she wanted to do!

After ensuring that Martha had all the preparations under control, Mary slipped out the door and hurried home. Sitting on a shelf was a decorative jar made from alabaster. This bottle of precious perfume had been given to her and she had been saving it for a special occasion. Mary tenderly picked it up and held it to her nose, hoping for a whiff of the fragrance captured inside.

Mary returned with her prized possession and as she entered the door, all eyes turned to her. The dinner had already begun, and Martha served the meal while Lazarus, Jesus and His disciples were seated around the table. It only took one look at the elaborately decorated jar in her hands for all to recognize that it held expensive perfume. Impulsive and emotional Mary . . . what was she up to? Though Mary was known to be demonstrative, they certainly did not expect what happened next.

Mary struck the neck of the jar against the table, releasing a powerful scent. She approached Jesus and without a word poured the contents of the entire bottle on His head and feet, the potent aroma filling the house. And then, with an expression of humility and devotion to her Lord, Mary kneeled before Him and began wiping His feet with her hair.

The guests were astonished at this outlandish demonstration and the disciples started grumbling angrily. Oh, to be sure, the culture required anointing the head of a guest with oil, washing his feet and giving a kiss, but wasn't this overdoing it? The grumbling intensified to harsh rebuke with the men chastising Mary, not for being scandalous, but for being wasteful. Judas was the strongest objector. "The perfume is worth a year's wages! It could have been sold and the money given to the poor!"

Though Mary was not concerned about their opinions, she hesitated momentarily, concerned that her actions were ill-timed. She certainly had not intended to cause a scene and looked up to Jesus. His approving smile was all she needed to see.

JESUS LOOKED INTO HER HEART

Jesus was fully aware of the dynamics of this scene. On the one hand, His friend Mary had intentionally poured her treasure on His head and feet and was now humbly bowing before Him out of the deepest expression of a heart filled with gratitude and worship. On the other hand, His disciples were criticizing her for what they judged to be an inappropriate and wasteful action. All they could see was the monetary cost of the perfume, though presenting their scolding as a concern for the poor. Their accusing hearts spoke volumes and the contrast did not go unnoticed.

Jesus saw kneeling before Him a woman after God's own heart — transparent, genuine, devoted, surrendered and pure as the oil of spikenard used to anoint Him. Unlike many of the other women He had encountered, Mary's actions were not based on her unfulfilled needs, but on an overflowing desire to give to Him.

HIS RESPONSE

With perfume dripping from His head, He forcefully said to His disciples, "Leave her alone! Why are you bothering this woman?" Jesus stated that Mary had kept this perfume for the day of His burial and had done a beautiful thing for Him. Instead of condemning her, as the others had, Jesus commended her for this lovely act of kindness shown to Him before His anticipated death.

Jesus was not uncomfortable or embarrassed by this sincere display of devotion. He embraced her uninhibited expression of love. This was the second recorded time that a woman had poured oil over His feet and wiped them with her hair. What was perceived by the men in attendance as either scandalous or wasteful was affirmed by Jesus as an appropriate demonstration of worship and affection.

By defending Mary, Jesus implied that He too, placed a higher value on heartfelt worship than on physical possessions. Jesus did not disapprove of the use of physical possessions to help the poor, but expressed appreciation for the timing of Mary's adoration. Jesus reminded His disciples they would always have the poor with them, but He would not always be with them. Then He honored Mary by adding, "She did what she could do — in advance she poured perfume on My body to prepare it for My burial."

THE OUTCOME

Burial . . . Jesus had said it twice, confirming Mary's intuition of what was forthcoming! With the disciples quieted, she now was free to continue with wholehearted worship of her Lord, sharing intimacy with Jesus, knowing that any remaining time spent with Him was precious.

Mary placed her entire focus and identity in Jesus, unconcerned with the viewpoint of others or the cost of the perfume. Her relationship with Jesus demonstrated total belief in and dependence on Him. Mary gave Jesus her all — holding nothing back in communicating her reverence and devotion. And Mary gave Jesus her best — the best of her time, the best of her resources and the best of her heart. Every moment with Jesus counted. He was completely the focus of her being, and she loved Him with all her heart, soul, mind and strength.

Most important of all, because of Mary's extravagant expression of adoration, Jesus proclaimed that the story of the beautiful thing she did for Him during a dinner in the town of Bethany would be told throughout the world, in her memory.

"Therefore, everyone who will acknowledge Me before men, I will also acknowledge him before My Father in heaven."

Matthew 10:32 HCSB

One Final Act of Kindness

Standing by the cross of Jesus were His mother, His mother's sister, Mary the wife of Clopas, and Mary Magdalene. When Jesus saw His mother and the disciple He loved standing there, He said to His mother, "Dear woman, this man is now your son," and to the disciple, "She is now your mother." And from that time on, the disciple took her into his own home.

DEAR WOMAN, HERE IS YOUR SON.

JOHN 19:25-27

79

THE SCENE

"Mary, come quickly! They are going to crucify Jesus!" The ordeal had begun. She had already been awake throughout the night after reports of His arrest, and she was confident He would be found innocent of any wrongdoing and released. But crucified? There must be some mistake! Initially, Mary was frantic, but she silently prayed for peace. Her challenge had always been to navigate between being the human mother of Jesus and the mother of God's Son. It had been difficult to temper her maternal inclinations and emotional viewpoint with the knowledge that Jesus was the Son of God who had a divine appointment and mission that she did not clearly understand.

Accompanied by her friends, she hurried through the streets while moving toward the rancorous noise that filled the air. The streets were lined with people shaking their fists and spitting at the three men trudging along the cobblestone pathway. Each man labored under the weight of a cross he was required to carry to the crucifixion site. How could this be? One of the men was her Jesus! A wave of nausea overcame Mary, and the women held her tightly when her knees buckled. She felt faint.

Mary could not even begin to grasp the level of hatred and cruelty that would bring humans to treat others like this. None of this made any sense to her, but there was no way to escape the horrific reality of the circumstances. Her son was about to die, through no fault of His own. No, no! They have it all wrong! Don't they know that this is God's very own Son — her son? The cursing and feverish shouting drowned out her cries as she watched Jesus stumble and fall. The soldiers grabbed a man from the crowd and forced him to carry Jesus' cross.

On they trudged, one grueling step after the other, until they reached Golgotha. Mary refused to watch as each of Jesus' hands was nailed to the cross beam. She covered her ears to block out the screams when the nails went through His feet and the cross was hoisted into an upright position.

Words cannot begin to describe the physical and emotional condition of Mary as she followed the crucifixion procession of Jesus through the streets of Jerusalem and to the foot of the cross that constrained Him. Though she was consumed with grief at watching her son suffer, the depth of her feelings was intensified because of the exceptional bond she had with this condemned man. From Jesus' conception by the Holy Spirit, their relationship was anything but normal. Although Mary was mother to additional children, Jesus was undeniably special.

Only a woman of internal strength and divine guidance could have dealt with her God-given assignment. As Jesus' mother, Mary's life had already been complicated. She courageously persevered during a scandalous virgin pregnancy. After giving birth in a less than desirable stable, she made a hasty escape to Egypt, protecting her son from raging King Herod. These sacrifices she knowingly and willingly made, trusting God's promises that had been spoken to her by an angel.

Mary knew her son had a unique destiny because the angel told her to name her baby Jesus, meaning "The Lord saves." But nothing had prepared her for this final scene. Jesus' face was barely recognizable after the brutal beating and scourging He had received at the hands of the Romans. Sure, He was a grown man, but this was her firstborn son. Treasured memories of His special childhood came to her mind. What a joy Jesus had been! He brought so much life into their home with His curious and creative nature. She remembered the lessons at the kitchen table as Scriptures were learned and discussed. Even as a young boy, He paid special interest to those who were disadvantaged, defending the disabled against the cruel remarks of bullies. She would beam with pride when neighbors would comment on His kindness, compassion and wisdom.

Quiet moans brought her back to reality. This was her own dear son, nailed to a cross, doomed to die. How precious Jesus was to her.

Though they shared a close mother-to-son relationship, Mary knew she eventually had to share Jesus with the world and had mixed feelings about His growing independence. She had a flashback to a frantic three-day search for Jesus when He was twelve years old. They found Him in the temple courts sitting among the teachers engaged in discussion, confident of His decision to be "in His Father's house."

As He grew in height and strength from carpentry work with her husband Joseph, Jesus also seemed to become increasingly moved by the injustices and suffering He witnessed. The passion in His voice and fire in His eyes intrigued Mary as she waited for signs of His prophesied power. The bond of a mother would naturally be intense, but coupled with the divine circumstances of His conception and prophetic mission, Mary watched Him with admiration, maybe even with curiosity. So when the wine ran out during the wedding festivities they were attending in the village of Cana, she approached Jesus, anticipating a display of His miraculous power. She had an inkling of His destiny and believed in Him, telling the servants, "Do whatever He tells you!" His first public miracle of changing water into wine confirmed what she had held in her heart for years.

Mary had watched from a distance as Jesus fully engaged in ministry by healing the sick, restoring sight to the blind, teaching and providing food for the masses. She too, was awed by the miracles, but was the only person in the crowd who could say to herself, "That's my son!" Though Jesus' focus was always on His mission, He always seemed to be aware of her presence and there continued to be a special connection when their eyes met. It still was difficult to let go and allow Him to fulfill His prophetic role, whatever that was to mean. Mary understood His ministry of miracles as confirmation of His identity as the Son of God. But she had no hint of the intense suffering He would face — the public ridicule, eventual arrest, scourging and now this sentence of death via crucifixion.

It seemed so surreal, but there she stood watching this man die. While others loved Jesus because of the roles He played in their lives, such as Teacher and Healer, she saw this man through a mother's eyes. This man was her adored child. It also seemed so final. She could barely stand, as she was exhausted, numbed with shock and grief. Her sorrow was overwhelming. Maybe this is what Simeon meant when he spoke over her eight-day-old Jesus at the temple — "A sword will pierce your own soul, too."

She was confused. How could He be the Messiah, the Son of God, while nailed to a cross? Though she did not understand, Mary trusted God just as she had done when the angel appeared to her announcing she would be the one to bring God's Son into the world. And she knew that whatever happened was according to God's plan — His will for Jesus and for her.

Every now and then, Mary would look up to Jesus and offer Him a weak smile. The end must be near. Is He really going to leave me? How can this be possible that I'm losing my son? I must stay strong for Him. Heavenly Father, she pleaded, this is more than I can bear.

Mary was grateful for her friends who were supporting her through this darkest day of her life. The empathetic disciple John reassured her with his gentle strength and comforting touch.

Jesus cleared His voice, as if attempting to speak, and Mary looked up into His face.

Jesus Looked Into Her Heart

Looking down from the cross at His mother, He understood the anguish she was enduring. This woman, the one who had carried Him in her womb after conception by the Holy Spirit and given Him birth, could barely look at Him because watching Him suffer was emotionally catastrophic.

But He also knew that just as her pain during childbirth was replaced by joy at the arrival of a son, in a matter of days her current sorrow would also turn to joy upon His appearance as the risen Christ. Of course, she could not see the outcome and was experiencing a mother's most terrifying agony — witnessing the suffering of her child, her Jesus.

Yes, Jesus understood the intense maternal bond that endured even when that child grew into manhood. He loved her so. She was His mother — the most significant woman in His life. She had devotedly been by His side from day one. Even after He publicly seemed to distance Himself from His family by claiming "whoever does God's will is My brother and sister and mother," she continued to love and follow Him.

Jesus also understood she would soon be alone and miss Him dearly. So, as He looked into His mother's heart, grieving at her impending loss, He determined to honor her and make provision for her care.

His Response

"Dear woman, this is your son." Though Jesus spoke with halted breath, the tone of gratitude and admiration for His mother was clear to those within earshot. The man by Mary's side, His close friend and disciple John, was now to stand in place of her son Jesus.

To His friend He said, "Here is your mother," indicating that from that point forward John would take the previously widowed Mary into His home and provide for her — in Jesus' place.

Jesus knew John was uniquely gifted with the ability to love and that His mother would be well cared for while living in his household. John had supported Mary throughout this trying time and would be able to provide for her physical and emotional needs the rest of her days. John would also be able to offer the special love that only a son can give to his mother. Jesus entrusted John to ensure Mary's status and reputation would be upheld with dignity, knowing that public scrutiny associated with His trial and death would be intense.

So, Jesus' final act of compassion was reserved for His own dear mother — the one woman selected to bear, nurture and raise the Son of God. While taking on the sins of the entire world, Jesus still had the presence of mind to focus on one woman, His mother.

THE OUTCOME

Even though He was in excruciating agony, Jesus was concerned for the hearts of others, specifically His mother's, with her cries of grief. He looked down on this blessed woman, His mother Mary, and honored her by ensuring she would be safe, provided for and treated with loving kindness because of her significant role in His life.

Soon after His comforting words, Jesus let out a loud cry and breathed His last breath. It was finished! A terrifying earthquake punctuated the pivotal moment in history. After a soldier jabbed a spear in His side, Mary remained to watch His lifeless body taken down from the cross. She followed as He was laid in a tomb. A large stone was rolled over the entrance and those gathered paused to grasp the finality of the moment. After lingering by His grave, Mary went home with John, drained and empty. Only time would be able to resolve her seemingly hopeless situation.

She DID see her Jesus again, this time as the resurrected Son of God, the world's Savior! Oh, the joy of their reunion! All was well! However, Mary would continue to miss His presence — seeing His smiling face, hearing His voice, feeling His embrace — after He ascended to heaven (Acts 1:9). The big picture was now clear, and she felt extremely blessed to have been Jesus' mother.

Jesus understands the heart of a mother when she has to witness her child suffering. He hears the cries of a mother's heart when a child is ill, hurting or in distress. He also understands that the trials in our present reality are nothing to be compared with the promise of a glorious eternity with Him. Yes, Jesus understands and He is kind.

"YOUR HEART MUST NOT BE TROUBLED. BELIEVE IN GOD; BELIEVE ALSO IN ME. IN MY FATHER'S HOUSE ARE MANY DWELLING PLACES; IF NOT, I WOULD HAVE TOLD YOU. I AM GOING AWAY TO PREPARE A PLACE FOR YOU. IF I GO AWAY AND PREPARE A PLACE FOR YOU, I WILL COME BACK AND RECEIVE YOU TO MYSELF, SO THAT WHERE I AM YOU MAY BE ALSO."

John 14:1-3 HCSB

Encounter with the Risen Jesus

It was preparation day, and the Sabbath was about to begin. The women who had come with Him from Galilee followed along and saw the tomb and how His body was laid in it. Mary Magdalene and Mary the mother of Joses were watching where He was placed. Then they returned and prepared spices and perfumes. And they rested on the Sabbath according to the commandment.

Early on the first day of the week, while it was still dark, Mary Magdalene went to the tomb and saw that the stone had been rolled away from the entrance. So she ran to Simon Peter and the other disciple, the one Jesus loved, and said, "They have taken the Lord out of the tomb, and we don't know where they have put Him!"

Mary stood outside the tomb crying. As she wept, she bent over to look into the tomb and saw two angels inside. They were dressed in white and were sitting where Jesus' body had been. One was at the head and the other was at the foot. They asked, "Woman, why are you crying?" "They have taken away my Lord," she said, "and I don't know where they have put Him." Having said this, she turned around and saw Jesus standing there, but she did not realize that it was Jesus.

Who Is It You Are Looking For?

"Woman," Jesus said to her, "Why are you crying? Who is it you are looking for?" Thinking He was the gardener, she said, "Sir, if you have carried Him away, just tell me where you have put Him, and I will go and take Him away."

Jesus said to her, "Mary!" Turning around, she cried out in Aramaic, "Rabboni!" (which means Teacher). Jesus said, "Don't cling to Me, for I have not yet returned to the Father. Go instead to My brothers and tell them that I am returning to My Father and your Father, to My God and your God." Mary Magdalene went and announced to the disciples, "I have seen the Lord!" And she told them what He had said to her.

Very early on the first day of the week, after Jesus had risen to life, He appeared first to Mary Magdalene, out of whom He had driven seven demons. She went and told those who had been with Him and who were mourning and weeping. Even though they heard that Jesus was alive and had been seen by her, they would not believe it.

MARK 15:47, 16:9-11
LUKE 23:55-56, 24:1-11
JOHN 20:1-2, 11-18

THE SCENE

Mary Magdalene sat outside Jesus' tomb weeping with despair. It was not supposed to have happened this way, or so she thought. Jesus had told His followers He would be going away, but this was not how she had imagined it.

Jesus was her Teacher and Master, and she had given Him everything — her livelihood and her heart. Along with other women, Mary Magdalene followed him from town to town, supporting His traveling group with money and supplies. So totally committed to serving Him, she was not concerned about her reputation. Many would try to paint her as an immoral woman with a romantic interest in Jesus. Yes, she knew people gossiped about her, but she also knew the truth. Oh, He was so much more than a man! Jesus was her Lord, the Son of God and the Messiah, chosen to save and redeem His people. Her reverence and awe of Jesus laid the foundation for the spiritual intimacy with Him that few understood or shared.

Something had drawn Mary to Jesus. It was His message that initially convicted her heart — a message of forgiveness, justice, redemption and hope. His message was in stark contrast to the abuse she had suffered in her life. Whereas people had treated her with contempt, Jesus spoke with respect and kindness.

Her belief in Him was strengthened as she witnessed miracles such as restoring sight to the blind and healing long standing infirmities and deformities. Mary had, in fact, been the recipient of a healing miracle herself, as Jesus released her from the suffering of being possessed by seven demons. No longer was she tormented by evil spirits and considered an outcast. Few understood the bondage of demon possession, the mental anguish and self-destructive behavior. But Jesus had graciously redeemed her from a bottomless pit and made her whole. Yes, she followed this man out of gratitude for the mercy He had extended to her. He had set her free and restored her life.

Mary's devotion to Jesus was not only due to the healing she received from Him. She came to believe in him as Truth — by listening to His parables and confrontations with Pharisees and by observing His example of compassion, mercy and forgiveness.

Mary loved being in His presence and faithfully stayed by the side of this condemned man named Jesus, who was scorned, beaten and crucified. Waves of grief had overwhelmed her as she watched His brutal and ignominious death on a cross. Joseph of Arimethea had provided a grave for Jesus' lifeless body. She watched as men lifted His corpse into the tomb and rolled a massive stone across the doorway. Mary returned to her home after His hasty burial, completely emotionally spent.

When the Sabbath was over, Mary Magdalene and other women headed for the tomb outside the city walls. They walked in a dazed motion, drained from the emotional upheaval of the past week's events, and brought sweet spices to complete the anointing process. As Mary entered the garden, she saw signs of the soldiers' post, including a smoldering fire and scattered equipment. But why had the stone been removed from the entrance? Weren't the guards posted there to keep watch over the sealed tomb?

Looking inside the tomb, she saw nothing, just the strips of linen that had bound her Lord. Not only had Mary's hopes been shattered with the death and burial of her beloved Jesus, but now His body was gone. Grave robbers! Frantically, she ran to tell Peter someone had taken the Lord's body.

Peter and others raced to the gravesite to see firsthand if

what Mary said was true. After confirmation of her story, they left, leaving her alone with her bewildered thoughts. So there she sat, sobbing inconsolably. Her loss was devastating. "Will I ever see Jesus again? I miss Him so."

Not knowing where to turn, Mary decided it was time to go back home. She stood up and took one last look into the tomb. Two angels were now sitting on the cold slab where Jesus had been placed. "Woman, why are you crying?" they asked. Dejected and seemingly unfazed by their presence, Mary told them, "They took my Lord and I don't know where they have put Him."

Mary turned around and saw a man standing there. She was unaware it was Jesus.

JESUS LOOKED INTO HER HEART

Jesus looked through the eyes and into the heart of one of His courageous followers whom He knew so well. Mary Magdalene was special in many ways — grateful, faithful, committed and wholehearted. She had endured much ridicule in her life, first from being demon possessed and also when accompanying Him as He traveled from town to town. He had heard the wagging tongues and accusations hurled at her. Though it was considered scandalous for a woman to be in the company of men, He knew the purity of her devotion to Him. He also understood the depth of her loss. Her heart was breaking because of her love for Him.

HIS RESPONSE

"Woman, why are you crying? Who is it you are looking for?" Mary was still dazed by the events of the past three days and thinking He was the gardener, asked Him to tell her where the body was so that she could go get it herself.

"Mary!" She snapped out of her stupor when her name was called and looked intently at the face of this man. "Mary!" He had spoken her name! His voice sounded familiar. Could it be? This man spoke with the same warmth and loving tone that she had come to know while conversing with Jesus on their travels. Yes, she recognized that voice! It was Jesus — "Teacher!"

The change in her countenance was dramatic as she burst into a radiant smile. She could not contain her joy and rushed to cling to Him, a natural response of adoration and an indication of their comfortable relationship. Gently, He said, "Don't hold on to Me for I have not returned to My Father." Then He commissioned her to tell His followers of His resurrection and that He was going back to "My Father and your Father, to My God and your God."

THE OUTCOME

What a profound encounter this was! It gave Jesus great joy to reveal Himself as the resurrected Christ first to a woman dogged by a negative reputation. All the more striking, as this was during a time when women could not be used as witnesses in legal proceedings, Jesus entrusted a woman with His message. So, of all His followers, Mary Magdalene was blessed to be the first person to say the words, "I have seen the Lord!"

No longer distraught, Mary was elated and raced to tell His disciples the good news. Initially they did not believe her, but soon they would also see their risen Lord, speak with Him and touch Him. No other event in the history of mankind has had such a significant outcome. Mary's jubilant proclamation, "I have seen the Lord!" changed everything and set world events on a new course.

Oh, there would be false witnesses bribed to claim that this historic event was staged and the body was stolen by His disciples.

But Mary would testify otherwise. She, along with numerous others would risk their lives as witnesses to the truth of this good news — that Jesus once confirmed dead, was now confirmed alive!

For Mary Magdalene, this good news, this great news, revolved around a fairly simple story of who this man Jesus was. He was the Son of God born as prophesied of a virgin, Mary, whom she personally knew. His ministry proclaimed love, forgiveness, redemption, healing and hope for all humanity.

Jesus demonstrated that He, as God's Son, had power over death, bringing back to life a widow's dead son and His friend Lazarus. And just as He foretold, that same power raised Him from His grave. Jesus' resurrection power confirmed the truth of all aspects of His message and ministry. Jesus was no mere mortal, and He had the authority and power to heal, forgive and save.

It all became clear to Mary. The improbable, impossible and unthinkable had truly taken place! Prophecies had been fulfilled. Jesus was Immanuel, God with us (Matthew 1:23). The Messiah had come, had died, had been raised after three days and three nights and now was with His heavenly Father. Yes, it was a true, compelling and simple story to tell. She was an eyewitness to His humanity and to His divinity, and she could not suppress her joy in the complete revelation of this truth. She personally had known this man and was witness to the fact that He overcame the grave, conquering death. Jesus was all He said He was — God's Son, the Truth, Bread of Life, The Way, the Resurrection and Life, Light of the World, True Vine, a King — the great I AM.

Mary also had a testimony of her personal encounter with Jesus. Her story, though indescribably amazing, was equally simple and easy to share. She, a sinner, broken and outcast, was reclaimed by Jesus' mercy, grace and unconditional love. As an individual, Mary Magdalene had experienced the totality of who Jesus was and is. Just as Psalm 103:3-5 claimed, she was the recipient of Jesus' benefits and was forgiven, healed, redeemed, valued and loved. She was blessed with an intimate relationship with Jesus that was different from a worldly love. Jesus loved her without any expectations and His was a sacrificial love.

Jesus appeared to His followers over a period of forty days and spoke about the Kingdom of God (Acts 1:3). Their gatherings were joyful occasions filled with praise and thanksgiving for this most extraordinary event — the resurrection of Jesus. Most likely, Mary Magdalene was there when His believers met together (Acts 1:14) while waiting expectantly to be baptized with the Holy Spirit (Acts 1:5, 8).

Life for Mary Magdalene changed the moment she encountered Jesus. She was blessed to be a personal eyewitness to His life, death and resurrection, and she lived out her remaining days full of the Holy Spirit and empowered to boldly share the message of hope for life in eternity with her Lord and Savior, her friend Jesus.

"And surely I am with you always, to the very end of the age."
Matthew 28:20 NIV

EPILOGUE

PORTRAIT OF YOUR ENCOUNTER WITH JESUS

The previous pages have provided stories of encounters women had with Jesus when He walked the dusty streets of Israel. These women personally met Jesus and experienced God in different ways. The nature of each interaction depended on the needs of the woman. Because each woman met Jesus in an intimate way, she was then able to share her personal story of how God had touched her life.

It is no different for us today, more than two thousand years after Jesus lived, died, rose from His grave and ascended to heaven. He also desires for us to know Him intimately and said He would always be with us. He sent the Holy Spirit to give us glimpses into His eternal love for us and to minister to us during those times when we do not see clearly.

What wonderful truth to know that we, too, can have a relationship with the God of the universe. We are loved and because of Jesus' sacrificial act on the cross we have been reconciled to our heavenly Father and will share eternity with Him. We may not see Jesus in the flesh as these women did, but through the Holy Spirit we can experience God in a variety of ways by which He reveals Himself — Deliverer, Comforter, Healer, Forgiver, Redeemer and Savior. Because "Jesus Christ is the same yesterday and today and forever" (Hebrews 13:8 NIV), we can be encouraged to know that He desires to relate to us personally just as He did with the women He met while on this earth.

JESUS UNDERSTOOD A WOMAN'S HEART

As the Creator of all, Jesus understood perfectly the inner workings of a human's body, mind and heart, as well as His original intent for males and females. He alone had the capacity to look into the innermost part of a woman's heart and to discern her needs and desires. Only Jesus had, and has, the ability to answer the central questions relating to a woman's identity: *Do I have value? Am I beautiful? Am I loved? Do I have a significant purpose? Am I safe?*

Jesus affirmed a woman's value. Jesus radically changed the perception of the value and worth of women by treating them with dignity, respect and as individuals of importance irrespective of their gender. His conduct toward women was in stark contrast to that which so many women have experienced. Throughout history, women have been devalued, subjected to subservient status and abused. Women have been treated as possessions and have been taken advantage of physically and emotionally. In some cultures women have been perceived to be second-class citizens and denied personal rights similar to men. Jesus' revolutionary acknowledgment and interaction with women had an immediate and timeless impact on society as a gender class and on women as individuals.

Jesus commonly interacted with a woman as an individual, independent of the other roles she may have been playing. He did not work through a woman's husband or her father, but directly with her. On several occasions Jesus' encounter with a woman did relate to her role as a mother or widow. But His response, whether with personal healing or healing for her child, was given as a direct reflection of the desire of her unique heart. Each woman was valued for who she was as a person, with her own identity, and Jesus responded to her needs or desires in a personal way.

Jesus valued emotional expression and demonstrated that a woman's heart responds to unconditional love. Jesus understood that at the core of a woman's heart is a longing to be loved for who she is as a uniquely created person. He did not trivialize or minimize her emotions and was comfortable when a woman tearfully shared the depths of her heart. He even seemed to encourage her emotional vulnerability by listening to her and honoring her requests while quieting any objections by observers.

Jesus did not condemn. Jesus loved a woman regardless of her human failings, sins and history of mistakes. Though never condoning a life outside the eternal will of the Father, neither did He condemn. Jesus did, however, influence those around Him to a higher calling of eternal perspective, continuing to show unfailing love when humans stumbled.

Jesus gave significance to women through recognition of their role as participants in His ministry, even allowing them to travel at times with His "ministry team." Women supported Him financially and many women stood courageously by Jesus at the cross (Matthew 27:55). The significance Jesus gave to women was underscored by the fact that He revealed Himself as the risen Christ first to a woman. Jesus also affirmed the timeless values of trust, faithfulness, belief and compassion that women exhibited. Though many of these women were unnamed in the Bible and without social status, He used their humanly insignificant lives as examples of eternal worth.

Jesus provided the ultimate security. Jesus was concerned when a woman was not provided for, and especially for the plight of widows. Because He understood a woman's need to feel secure physically, emotionally and spiritually, His encounters with those who needed security resulted in a sense of emotional comfort and safety. Through Jesus' death and resurrection, He provided the ultimate security. Many women sensed that though poor, destitute or devalued in the eyes of society, they were eternally safe and confidently waited for their place in Jesus' Kingdom.

Jesus loved unconditionally by grace. He loves you too, unconditionally, not because of what you can offer and give to Him, but because He loves and values you for who you are. Jesus places you in high esteem — regardless of the level of worth society may ascribe to you. He paid the price for your redemption with the ultimate sacrifice of His life, bestowing on you value, worth and regard. Remember that you are His Creation! That is the spiritual foundation you are assured of and upon which you can build.

Jesus came to save, restore and give life. As Creator, it certainly was not Jesus' intent for a woman to be abused, suffer, be alone, feel insecure, worthless or insignificant. But because she, along with the human race, had fallen from the original intent, Jesus would fill other relational roles in her life — Savior, Redeemer, Friend, Defender, Protector and Bridegroom.

Jesus was sent to earth by His and our heavenly Father so that each of us could have life to the full and live in freedom through an intimate relationship with Him. Because Jesus came to earth in human form, He relates to our humanity and meets our individual needs in a way that speaks to our unique circumstances and hearts. He alone can provide for our physical, emotional and spiritual needs. Only He understands each of us personally and has the ability and power to restore and complete us.

JESUS LOVED WOMEN THEN AND LOVES WOMEN NOW

Through the various portraits that have been presented, we have a more complete understanding of who Jesus is and His purpose — to save and give life to all humanity. Just as with the women of the Bible, Jesus pursues you out of the crowd, understands your background and situation. He knows your name and desires to comfort you in times of stress and uncertainty. He is eager to forgive, redeem and save. Jesus will never give up on you, never think less of you and never condemn.

Every woman consciously or unconsciously experiences a deep longing for spiritual intimacy, asking God, "Do you know me? Are you concerned about the issues on my heart? Can I trust you? Will you love me unconditionally?" Even though our human relationships may be flawed or have failed, we can always be assured of intimacy with a perfect and unfailing God.

Dear woman, Jesus will not abandon you — He has unlimited patience, compassion and empathy. He longs to be your friend (John 15:15) and share all aspects of your life — your ups, downs, joys and challenges. How comforting it is to know "You have looked deep into my heart, Lord, and you know all about me" (Psalm 139:1 CEV). In other words, He divinely loves YOU!

WOMEN PURSUED JESUS

We have seen examples of women who were compelled and determined to seek Jesus out. Some had physical needs, some spiritual needs and some were drawn to His message of hope. Their examples are intended to encourage you to diligently seek Jesus — pursue Him, learn from Him, surrender to Him, listen to Him and ask Him to complete you. "For everyone who asks receives; he who seeks finds; and to him who knocks, the door will be opened" (Luke 11:10 NIV).

Remember that Jesus Himself said, "Come to Me" (Matthew 11:28). Therefore, similar to the phrase in Psalm 17:15 you can confidently ask, "But my prayer, in righteousness, is to see Your face, your likeness; on waking, may I be satisfied with a vision of You and Your presence." In essence, you are seeking and asking to have a new discovery of the Person and work of Jesus Christ — an encounter with God.

Faith is required to trust and to surrender to God. Do you fear those times when He looks into the darkest places in your heart and life? Or do you doubt that you are worthy to be loved by Him? You must believe that Jesus is the only way to find the solutions to your problems. He is the only One who can give you living water to quench the thirst of your heart, the only One who knows the truth of what God's will is for your life.

There may be times when God seems silent or distant, but just as the mother respectfully persisted in her pleas, be encouraged to keep moving forward toward Him and wait for His timing. Continue to be open-hearted and ready to hear His voice when He calls. "Draw near to God, and He will draw near to you" . . . "Humble yourselves before the Lord, and He will exalt you" (James 4:8, 10 HCSB).

YOUR PERSONAL ENCOUNTER

Because God loves you and desires to have an intimate and eternal relationship with you, expect to have an encounter with Him. In fact, as you continue to come to Him and pursue Him, expect many encounters with Him. As you seek and become aware of God's presence in your life, you will experience Him in ways that uniquely touch your heart, providing your own story and testimony of God's irresistible goodness to share with others.

Jesus will not leave you alone or forsake you. He is actively seeking you and desires for you to experience the many roles He plays in your life. Just as Psalm 103:3-5 describes, you may experience Him as God who heals, God who forgives, God who redeems, God who crowns with love and righteousness, God who satisfies your desires, God who restores. Maybe you will experience Him as God who dances, God who comforts and God who counsels. During your journey with Jesus you will experience Him through a variety of ways that will be unique and personal to you.

Maybe your encounter will come from one of His words in Scripture, or from a word of encouragement from one of His followers, or through the lyrics of a song. Your encounter may come in the form of a direct answer to prayer or an open door that speaks of God's goodness and personal involvement in your life. A direct word spoken, a vision or a miraculous delivery could be other ways that you might experience God's intervention in your life.

The portrait of your encounter will capture the moment when Jesus looked through your eyes into the depths of your heart and saw a need or desire, and then responded to you. Maybe you are lonely, are grieving, or need a rescue or release from guilt. Only God understands your deepest thoughts, desires and needs that are expressed in your heart. When He answers, you will know you have intimately encountered Him. Each of your portraits will tell how God revealed Himself personally to you, so you may experience His unlimited love.

An encounter with Jesus brings joy and a deep sense of peace, knowing that He has answered one of your central identity questions — Do you love me? Am I beautiful in Your eyes? Do I have value? Do I have a significant purpose? Am I safe?

As you experience a powerful God in a personal way, it is helpful to chronicle your various portraits so that you may remember the details of each event. What was it about the encounter that specifically addressed your need or desire of your heart? How did God intimately reveal Himself to you? As you periodically review your journal, you will see how God's hand has faithfully been on your life, confirming that His love for you is consistent and His timing is perfect. These personal encounters deepen your relationship with God and your heart will overflow with praise, adoration and worship for your indescribably amazing God.

Dear woman, may you be blessed with continual encounters with your Lord and Savior — your friend, Jesus.

"THIS IS ETERNAL LIFE: THAT THEY MAY KNOW YOU, THE ONLY TRUE GOD, AND THE ONE YOU HAVE SENT — JESUS CHRIST."
John 17:3 HCSB

ABOUT THE AUTHOR

Barbara Quillen Egbert credits her life experiences — in the roles as a wife, mother, published author, educator, camp director and ministry leader — as the foundation to her interest in and understanding of women's identity issues as they relate to God's original intent for their lives.

One of her most fulfilling roles was that of camp director of the SEP Camp in Minnesota where she was lovingly nicknamed "Momma Egbert." It was during her involvement at the camp that she met the actor who portrayed Jesus in the Matthew film. Through Bruce Marchiano's portrayal and personal testimony, the author was given a glimpse of the zealous love Jesus has for each of God's children, inspiring her quest to relate heart-to-heart with Him.

Due to the insights gained through her spiritual journey, the author can confidently state that a woman's identity issues are primarily addressed through an intimate relationship with Jesus. Her interest in art combined with a personal encounter with Jesus provided the inspiration for the concept of the book — verbally and artistically capturing the portrait of a woman's unique encounter with Jesus.

As a ministry leader, she readily shares her journey of experiencing God and encourages others to seek their own personal relationship with Jesus. Her greatest joy is when others experience the love, restoration and peace found only in Him.

Born in Colorado, Barb has also lived in Iowa and Texas and now resides in California with her husband. She is blessed with three grown children and enjoys riding her cruiser bike along the beach, dancing, sailing, playing harp, tutoring young learners and walking through life with her friends. She loves exploring the coast of California in search of scenic places to write and experience God and His beautiful creation.

ABOUT THE ARTIST

Wilson Jay Ong grew up in the San Francisco Bay Area and received a BFA from Brigham Young University and afterward attended the Art Students' League. In addition to being a professional artist and illustrator since 1983, Wilson has taught art, presented workshops and exhibited his work nationally. He and his family currently live in Corning, New York.

"Concerning this project, I consider it a tremendous challenge and privilege to paint scenes from the life of the Savior. Nevertheless, it has been exciting to imagine, in particular, the tenderness with which He cared for the women in His life and others He came in contact with during His ministry."— Wilson Jay Ong